RENEWALS 458-4574

The Guide to Successful Destination Management

WITHDRAWN
UTSA LIBRARIES

The Wiley Event Management Series

SERIES EDITOR: DR. JOE GOLDBLATT, CSEP

WITHDRAWN
UTSA LIBRARIES

The Guide to Successful Destination Management

Pat Schaumann, CMP, CSEP, DMCP

**Endorsed and Approved by the Association
of Destination Management Executives (ADME)**

WILEY

JOHN WILEY & SONS, INC.

Library
University of Texas
at San Antonio

This book is printed on acid-free paper.♾

Copyright © 2005 by John Wiley & Sons, Inc. All rights reserved.

Published by John Wiley & Sons, Inc., Hoboken, New Jersey
Published simultaneously in Canada

No part of this publication may be reproduced, stored in a retrieval system, or transmitted in any form or by any means, electronic, mechanical, photocopying, recording, scanning, or otherwise, except as permitted under Section 107 or 108 of the 1976 United States Copyright Act, without either the prior written permission of the Publisher, or authorization through payment of the appropriate per-copy fee to the Copyright Clearance Center, Inc., 222 Rosewood Drive, Danvers, MA 01923, (978) 750-8400, fax (978) 646-8600, or on the web at www.copyright.com. Requests to the Publisher for permission should be addressed to the Permissions Department, John Wiley & Sons, Inc., 111 River Street, Hoboken, NJ 07030, (201) 748-6011, fax (201) 748-6008.

Limit of Liability/Disclaimer of Warranty: While the publisher and author have used their best efforts in preparing this book, they make no representations or warranties with respect to the accuracy or completeness of the contents of this book and specifically disclaim any implied warranties of merchantability or fitness for a particular purpose. No warranty may be created or extended by sales representatives or written sales materials. The advice and strategies contained herein may not be suitable for your situation. You should consult with a professional where appropriate. Neither the publisher nor author shall be liable for any loss of profit or any other commercial damages, including but not limited to special, incidental, consequential, or other damages.

For general information on our other products and services or for technical support, please contact our Customer Care Department within the United States at (800) 762-2974, outside the United States at (317) 572-3993 or fax (317) 572-4002.

Wiley also publishes its books in a variety of electronic formats. Some content that appears in print may not be available in electronic books. For more information about Wiley products, visit our web site at www.wiley.com.

Library of Congress Cataloging-in-Publication Data:

Schaumann, Pat.
  The guide to successful destination management / Pat Schaumann.
    p. cm. — (The Wiley event management series)
    ISBN 0-471-22625-4 (Cloth)
  1. Hotel concierges. 2. Special events—Management. 3. Tourism—Management.   I. Title. II. Series.
  TX911.3.C63S33   2004
  647.94′068—dc22

2003016877

Library
University of Texas
at San Antonio

Printed in the United States of America.

10 9 8 7 6 5 4 3 2 1

The officers and directors of the Association of Destination Management Executives (ADME) respectfully dedicate *The Guide to Successful Destination Management* to the pioneers of the industry, who realized the need for support services for those planning meetings, conferences, and events.

Contents

Foreword

The term *logistics* is derived from the Greek word *logos,* which means "reason." When meeting and event managers develop and execute the logistics for their events they must act reasonably. That is to say, they must, according to most legal opinions, "do what a reasonable person must do" to ensure a safe, secure, and successful event experience. Many meeting and event professionals will readily admit that when it comes to the complex logistics that are required for many programs, *destination management experts* are the masters of this important responsibility.

Although a relatively young field within event management, the destination management profession has quickly grown to encompass the transportation of millions of guests each year. A well-known NFL Super Bowl halftime producer once told me that the most critical aspect of the show was transporting the cast and crew to and away from the stadium. To handle this job, he relied on a local destination management company whose expertise and experience would ensure a successful outcome.

However, destination management companies provide far more than transportation. From tours to travel, from entertainment to local rules of etiquette, the destination management consultant is the premier local expert who can guide you to the right venue, location, resource, speaker, and vendor. The staff of these companies often represent hundreds of years of professional experience in a market area that may be unfamiliar to you. Therefore, by using their services you are not only saving significant time but also helping guarantee a better outcome.

From coordinating registration processes to creating and supervising a complex theme event, destination management professionals offer event managers one-stop shopping, which can reduce time required to organize the event and often trim costs. This book is the first complete guide to this important fact of the event management industry.

Through the pages of this book you will learn how to identify, select, work with, and evaluate destination management companies to benefit your guests as well as your organization. Whether you are planning a simple meeting for a board of directors or a major citywide event, this comprehensive book will provide you with the resources and steps needed to ensure that you succeed every time.

The author, Pat Schaumann, CSEP, CMP, DMCP, is one of the pioneers and leaders in the destination management industry. Ms. Schaumann not only is the founder of a successful destination management firm in St. Louis, Missouri, but is a popular speaker and well-respected industry author. This book has been endorsed by the leading organization of destination management professionals, the Association of Destination Management Executives, as their official guide to the profession.

The logistics for your next program deserve the precise, knowledgeable, and creative planning and execution that destination management professionals provide. For you to best benefit from their services, this book is a must read. This book is the single most powerful tool you can use to control the logistics for your event—to "act reasonably." Thanks to the excellent work of Pat Schaumann and her colleagues at the Association of Destination Management Executives the quality bar is rising worldwide for all events through the contributions of this important and valuable guide.

Dr. Joe Goldblatt, CSEP
Wiley Event Management Series Editor

Preface

An increasing number of people are participating in destination management, and there is every indication that this industry will continue to expand. Academic study of this industry is fairly recent and has not yet coalesced into a curriculum. Some academics, who could help guide those entering the industry or seeking to improve their competence, have emerged.

Those who are called upon to organize destination management services have had very few resources and training manuals to employ as reference. Although some limited sources are available for assistance, no one resource book comprehensively describes the process and offers thorough advice and guidance.

The lack of a complete resource and the need to provide a text resource for the *Destination Management Certified Professional* program is the main reason I decided to write this book. The evident need to provide an accurate training manual will also give the beginner a standard for better practice and procedure.

Special features of *The Guide to Successful Destination Management* include the sample forms, case study, and excerpted laws that appear in the appendixes.

There may be some repetition of content among chapters, which is unavoidable because destination management services interrelate and overlap.

Who Should Read This Book

The Guide to Successful Destination Management is written primarily for those who devote a major portion of their time to planning and arranging destination management. Many of these people are professionals who have experienced the challenges and processes described in this book.

This book is also written for the students within the industry. The book will enable them to understand what destination management companies do and how their services complete the production of successful meetings, events, and conferences.

Programs of the Association of Destination Management Executives

The Association of Destination Management Executives (ADME) is composed of organizations whose members are involved in and directly responsible for services provided by destination management companies. As the pre-eminent organization for Destination Management Executives, the mission is to increase the professionalism and effectiveness of destination management through member and industry education, to establish standard ethical practices, and to raise the level of awareness of the value of destination management to the respective association, at the corporate level or in the private sector.

The Destination Management Certified Professional Program

ADME has established a certification program, the Destination Management Certified Professional (DMCP), in order to create impetus for organizational self-improvement and to stimulate a general raising of standards.

The purpose of the DMCP program is to increase the professionalism within the destination management industry by establishing a level of knowledge and performance necessary for certification; identifying the body of knowledge required; stimulating the art and science of destination management; increasing the value of practitioners to their employers; recognizing and raising industry standards and practices, and, thereby, ethics; and maximizing the value of the products and services that certified destination management professionals can provide.

Acknowledgments

The decision to write this book was born from a group of dedicated professionals who recognized the need to create the first body of knowledge devoted to the destination management industry. Originating a book as in-depth as this one required an immense amount of time and energy. I wish to express my gratitude and heartfelt thanks to my family, staff, and friends, who supported this effort over a three-year period.

Many thanks to the destination management industry members who contributed their efforts to make this book possible and to the Association of Destination Management Executives who, in an effort to standardize good practice within the industry by creating a certification examination, drove the making of this book.

The following members of the Association of Destination Management Executives are the visionaries whose contributions to this book prove their dedication and inspiration to professionalism.

M. Ellis Frater, Jr., DMCP
President, Dietrich Destination Management, New Orleans, Louisiana

Susan Gray, DMCP
Executive vice president, MAC Meetings and Events, St. Louis, Missouri

Fabienne Hanks, CMP, DMCP
Vice president of Marketing and Sales, The Meeting Manager, San Diego, California

Trevor Hanks, CMP, DMCP
Director of sales, The Meeting Manager, Orange County, California

Christopher H. Lee, DMCP
President, ACCESS California

Diane Lyons, DMCP
President, Accent on Children's Arrangements, New Orleans, Louisiana

Peg Mahoney, CMP, DMCP
President, Showcase Associates, Philadelphia, Pennsylvania

Helen Moskovitz, DMCP
President, The Key Event & Helen Moskovitz Group, Nashville, Tennessee

Ilene Reinhart, CMP, DMCP
   President, ACCESS California, Southern California
Sylvia Rottman, DMCP
   President/CEO, Great Events/TEAMS, Inc., Denver,
   Colorado
Linda Simon, DMCP
   Executive vice president, The Best of Boston, Ltd., Boston,
   Massachusetts
Gordon Thompson, DMCP
   Partner, Cappa & Graham, Inc., San Francisco, California
Dorrit Turner, DMCP
   Owner/CEO, Yellow Rose Touring and Special Events,
   Dallas, Texas

Very special thanks to our wonderful publishing family, John Wiley & Sons, Inc., Hoboken, New Jersey. Thanks, also, to Dr. Joe Goldblatt, CSEP, for his inspirational and enthusiastic leadership in the hospitality industry. The growth and recognition of professionalism in our industry is a result of his passion for collegiate and educational programs.

Many thanks to Karen Giebel, MAC Meetings and Events, and Andrew Pelsma, University of Kansas, for their diligent efforts as reviewers, readers, and editorial assistants.

Heartfelt thanks to my company administrator and the DMCP certification administrator, Kimberly Rueter, for her ability to keep me on schedule and for her brilliance and time spent to ensure book content was accurate.

Loving thanks to my son, Michael Schaumann, whose editing expertise made the content flawless.

Thanks to my company management, who supported my time and effort to complete the arduous task of writing the book while still managing the business.

Many thanks to my husband, Dennis, daughter, Marissa, and son, Michael, who have long been accustomed to my long hours and remain lovingly supportive. It is through them that I have been able to achieve my lifelong goals and still be able to enjoy and treasure every quality minute of time that I share with them.

And finally to my mom, Rose Singrun, for a lifetime of inspiration and support.

Dedication to Professionalism

As is true for many emerging industries, people working in the field of destination management came to it by chance or were temporarily employed and elected to continue. We are confident that all people involved in destination management will benefit from the aggregation and organization of the numerous details required for successful destination management offered in this book.

Pat Schaumann, CMP, CSEP, DMCP
St. Louis, Missouri

The Guide to Successful Destination Management

CHAPTER 1

Understanding Destination Management

"I have been in the industry for over 20 years and have learned to rely on destination management companies for their expertise in their specific locations. They have assisted on many of my company meetings and our largest trade show, providing a list of services including ground transportation, shuttles, events, staff support, and many more. As a meeting professional, I recognize the value of the DMC industry and the professionalism and consistency that they bring to my programs."

BILL SEVERSON

MANAGER, MEETINGS & SPECIAL EVENTS

ROCKWELL AUTOMATION

IN THIS CHAPTER YOU WILL LEARN TO:

- Understand what destination management is.
- Demonstrate the ability to evaluate a destination management company using a checklist.
- Know the guidelines clients should use for selecting a destination management company.
- Consider the changing environment for destination management.

The History of Destination Management

In the beginning. . . . Sometime during the 1960s, as a response to meeting and convention planners' desire for custom group leisure activities during their programs, a new business was born. Referred to as **ground operators,** they were mostly small entrepreneurships operating in a single destination. These local companies offered basic services, including airport meet and greet, transportation, tours, and recreation (mainly golf) for groups.

In the 1970s, many of these companies added custom parties and themed events, as well as spouse/guest programs, to their list of services. The term *destination management* was coined in 1972 by Phil Lee, founder of California Leisure Consultants, to describe the expanded role they played as local **logistics** experts. Logistics is the procurement, maintenance, and transportation of material, equipment, and people. Marketing alliances such as The DMC Network and The Contact Group were formed by some of the early pioneers to provide networking and referrals within an exclusive group of destination management service providers.

During the economic boom of the 1980s, **destination management companies (DMCs)** flourished, further expanding their role in the meeting, convention, and incentive travel industry. New DMCs were popping up everywhere, bringing fierce competition to many markets. By the end of the decade, several regional and national destination management companies had emerged. As a 1991 *Successful Meetings* magazine cover story proclaimed, "A Cottage Industry Comes of Age!"

Then came the recession of the late 1980s and early 1990s, and with it a couple of major shifts. More companies were competing for fewer dollars. Organizations were forced to cut their meeting (recreation) budgets. Other suppliers like hotels, decorators, and transportation companies began offering similar services. Some DMCs began traveling with clients from destination to destination.

In the 1990s we witnessed for the first time aggressive expansion and "corporatizing" of the destination management business through industrial investment and venture capital. Mergers and acquisitions, joint ventures, cooperative marketing agreements, and even franchise offerings changed the face of destination management.

Today, destination management is a major industry, generating millions of dollars in revenue and employing thousands of people. See Figure 1-1 for the latest figures on this growing industry.

ASSOCIATION OF DESTINATION MANAGEMENT EXECUTIVES

June 1995 marked a significant milestone for DMCs, the formation of the **Association of Destination Management Executives (ADME).** This was recognition of destination management as more than a vocation, but a viable industry within an industry.

The Association of Destination Management Executives (ADME) conducts an annual survey to measure various segments of the industry. The following are the survey results based on responses from 500 destination management companies.

- ADME projects that the 500 to 1,000 DMCs in the United States generate **$1,002,043,000** annually in the hospitality/meetings and convention industry.
- Of the figures supplied, the following segments were purchasing items:
  Transportation $151,219,000
  Hotel Space (function space and event space) $126,600,000
- Average number of years ADME respondents have been in business: 19.2 years.
- 75 percent are the original owners of the company.
- Average number of employees for each company is 15.19.
- More than two thirds of the owners of responding companies have had at least 11 years of experience as a DMC.
- More than 50 percent of the owners had 20 years experience in the hospitality industry.
- Respondents reported that the 2001–2002 volume of business increased for 45 percent of those reporting and decreased for 36 percent of those reporting.
- Respondents ranked the most important issues currently facing them:
  1. In-house DMCs
  2. Clients requesting proposals then going directly to the suppliers themselves
  3. Industry awareness of DMCs
- Respondents listed the following benefits of belonging to a professional association (ADME):
  1. Increase in the professionalism and effectiveness of destination management through member and industry education
  2. The establishment of standard ethical practices
  3. The promotion of the value of the industry globally to the general public

Figure 1-1
Destination Management 2003 Survey

Formed as a nonprofit, nonpartisan, international trade association, ADME grew to more than 250 members by the year 2000. It is now a source for destination management information worldwide, and has become the spokesgroup for the destination management industry.

The Mission of ADME is as follows: "To increase the professionalism and effectiveness of destination management through education, promotion of ethical practices, and availability of information to the meeting, convention, and incentive travel industry, and the general public."

ADME defines a destination management company as "a professional services company, possessing extensive local knowledge, expertise, and resources, specializing in the design and implementation of events, activities, tours, transportation and program logistics."

This definition identifies the dual role the destination management company plays in both designing and implementing programs for their clients.

AN ANALOGY

Christopher H. Lee, DMCP, president of ACCESS California, uses the following analogy to explain the role of DMCs. "A DMC is like the architect, utilizing their unique knowledge and experience (of the destination) to design a *blueprint* that fulfills the meeting, convention, or incentive travel planner's needs and desires, optimizes the available resources, and adheres to the limitations and requirements of the area."

"A DMC is also like the general contractor who 'builds the building.' They possess the skills, resources and relationships to see the job through. They develop the bid, hire and manage their subcontractors, relate to all outside agencies for permits, insurance, and so on, manage the finances of the job, provide constant supervision on-site and overall project management."

Another analogy describing the role of the DMC is that of the person who attempts to add on to or remodel a house him- or herself in an effort to save money. Although a seemingly simple project, halfway through the person might lament that hiring professionals to do the job would have achieved a better result while saving both time and money.

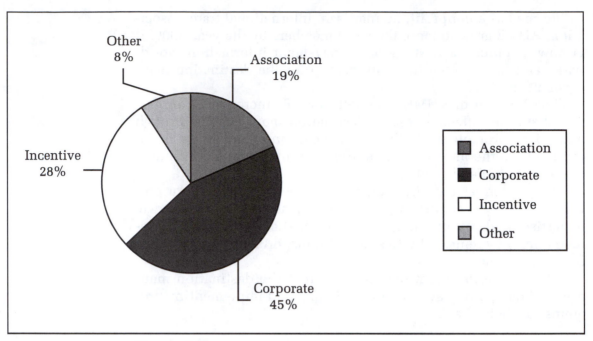

Figure 1-2
ADME DMC Survey—Breakdown by Client Type
Courtesy of the Association of Destination Management Executives

For meeting, convention, and incentive travel planners, the destination management company is that architect or builder! A good DMC designs and implements customized destination programs, based on its extensive local knowledge, saving the planner time and money, and producing a greater result. (See Figure 1-2 for a breakdown of the core markets for DMCs.)

The Role of Destination Management

This definition—professional services company, extensive local knowledge, design and implementation of events—is only a framework behind the important role that destination management plays. We need to examine what a DMC does to get a clearer picture.

A DMC gathers the information regarding a particular destination to support a client's needs. The list of services provided by a DMC may vary, but a true DMC can assist with site inspections and hotel rate negotiations; arrange for meet/greet services, ground transfers, and shuttle transportation; manage registration; provide support staff; create customized tours and companion programs; manage youth programs; arrange for events at unique venues; design and order gifts and amenities; provide total coordination of any type of event; design and produce props; and more. True DMCs are usually full-service, one-stop shops.

Because of their many local connections, DMCs can also provide entry into unique venues that might not normally be available for public use.

During program planning stages, DMCs maintain frequent client contact, imparting their creativity and thorough knowledge of their area to design a memorable program. Because clients depend on DMCs for their extensive local influence, DMCs are determined to have higher standards of competence and skills than those companies that provide single services.

The typical process of destination management starts well before the program. A number of pre-planning steps are involved. Destination management continues on site during the program and also includes post-program evaluation. DMCs are current on all local conditions, facilities, and program opportunities, thus enabling them to be the best contributors to a successful program. (See Figure 1-3 for a list of steps to keep in mind when planning a program.)

DMCs are synonymous with **professional conference organizers (PCOs).** PCOs are the international equivalent of DMCs in North America, although some regions call their service companies

---

1. Establish goals and objectives.
2. Assess the history of the program.
3. Target the demographics of the group.
4. Create a budget.
5. Design the program.
6. Negotiate contracts.
7. Establish a timeline.
8. Hire subcontractors.
9. Plan logistics.
10. Oversee program wrap-up.

Figure 1-3
Steps for Planning a Program

destination management companies, particularly within the Caribbean Islands. DMCs and PCOs offer total logistical planning in their locations. They offer a variety of services including, but not limited to, transportation, event management, and tours. PCOs were first established to support **incentive travel programs**—reward programs for employees based on their performance—and assist in conference planning and local interest programs. There are many **consortiums**—multiple-membered cultures (or natural assemblages) in which each organization meets for some definite purpose—or partnerships of both organizations serving as reference centers for service recommendations.

The **International Association of Professional Congress Organizers (IAPCO)** is a nonprofit organization, founded in 1968, that represents professional organizers and managers of international and national congresses, conventions, and special events. Along with the Association of Destination Management Executives, IAPCO is committed to raising standards of services among its members and other sectors of the meetings industry by means of continuing education and interaction with other professionals. IAPCO has members worldwide whose activities are monitored on an annual basis. As a result, IAPCO membership offers a unique quality assurance recognized by conference clients and suppliers all over the world.

The Association of Destination Management Executives (ADME) is a North American–based, nonprofit organization founded in 1995. It represents five classes of membership, including DMC executives, affiliates, associates, active, and emeritus. ADME sponsors and manages the only DMC certification program, the **Destination Management Certified Professional (DMCP),** which is a global professional designation based on experience and knowledge of the industry.

Evaluating DMCs

Qualifying a DMC should involve a comprehensive checklist:

- *Longevity:* Many companies open and close each year. A DMC that has existed for a long time has shown that its operation has a proven track record.

- *Financial stability:* Ask the DMC for the name of its bank, its **Dun & Bradstreet rating,** and a list of its major suppliers. Always follow up with any reference check. Dun & Bradstreet offers credit services and reports that let you check the business credit ratings of potential new customers before agreeing to credit terms. It also allows you to see if current customers, vendors, and suppliers are paying on time and be automatically notified of important changes in their credit ratings.
- *Client references:* Ask DMCs for a complete list of references, with particular emphasis on programs most similar to yours.
- *Basic company structure:* The DMC must have sufficient staff in order to deliver what it promises.
- *Insurance and risk management:* Assess the DMC's insurance and extent of staff training. What is the value of its liability insurance?
- *Computer technology:* Ask about its technology. What type of computers and software does it utilize? What are its full capabilities?
- *Professionalism:* In which professional organizations does the DMC maintain memberships? Is it active in the Association of Destination Management Executives (ADME), Meeting Professionals International (MPI), International Special Events Society (ISES), Society of Incentive & Travel Executives (SITE), Professional Convention Management Association (PCMA), or others? Does it belong to a DMC consortium? Does its staff have any industry certifications, such as **Certified Meeting Professional (CMP), Certified Special Event Professional (CSEP),** Destination Management Certified Professional (DMCP)?

Guidelines for Partnering with a DMC

Most meeting, convention, and incentive travel planners do not have the time or budget to personally research all of the possibilities and specifics for every destination being considered for their group's program(s). At best, they possess only basic knowledge of the destination(s) being considered. However, many organizations expect the planner to be an expert in every aspect of every destination.

The process of selecting a DMC to assist you in designing and implementing events, activities, tours, transportation, and program logistics for your group should be thorough. Not partnering with a DMC, or partnering with the wrong DMC, can negatively affect your entire program.

IDENTIFY CANDIDATES

Use the following methods to identify the right DMC for your program:

- Rely on word of mouth. Ask your peers and colleagues who they have worked with successfully in the destination/region where your program will be held.
- Check with the Association of Destination Management Executives (www.adme.org). The most professional DMCs are members.
- Ask the convention/visitor's bureau in the city or cities where your program will be for their *three* top DMC recommendations.
- Check the membership directories of professional associations you belong to, such as Meeting Professionals International, the Society of Incentive Travel Executives, American Society of Association Executives, or others.
- Ask the hotel you are working with for its top *three* recommendations, as well. Make sure (by asking) that the hotel is not paid or commissioned by the "recommended" DMC(s).
- Compare your results to see which DMC(s) stand out.

NARROW THE FIELD

Select two or three finalists based on the answers to the following questions: How long has the firm been in business? Is it a licensed business? Does it have permanent professional offices? How many full-time employees work for the company? What is the experience level of the employees who will manage your program(s)? Are its company values and individual personalities compatible with yours? Who will be on site during your program(s)? Can they be reached after hours?

In addition, ask to preview their contract terms up front. Require proof of adequate insurance coverage. A minimum of

$2 million coverage is standard. Ask for proof that their vendors are adequately insured, as well. Request a list of references that you can contact with programs similar to yours in size and scope.

Once you have identified your DMC finalists, notify those DMC firms not chosen and thank them for their efforts.

PROGRAM DESIGN

Give your finalist(s) all the group particulars:

- Group demographics (age range, male/female ratio, etc.)
- Specific interests/activities
- Program agenda/time constraints
- Past program information/history
- Program budget

Specify what services you want them to include in their proposal:

- Meet & greet/airport transfers
- Shuttle/transportation services
- Tours and recreation
- Special events/parties
- Dining arrangements
- Gifts and amenities
- Other services

If you require shuttle services, make sure that your finalist(s) are using the same criteria, in order to make a like comparison.

- Number of passengers assumed
- Quality and quantity of vehicles
- Proposed routes
- Average passenger wait times
- Number of staff included (on vehicles?)
- Quality and quantity of signage on vehicles and along route(s)
- Shuttle experience of bidders
- Group patterns/history

If you will be including tours and recreation in your program, provide your finalist(s) with the following information:

- Dates and times your group is available for tours and recreation
- Whether the activities be hosted or the individuals will pay

- What kind of recreation you want: on-property, off-property, educational, adventure, sporting, team building
- Whether you wish to include spouses or guests in the recreational activities
- Whether lunch or dinner should be included in the activities

If your program will include special events, ask your finalist(s) the following:

- How much experience does the DMC have producing special events?
- What events has the DMC created (similar to yours)? Check references and request photos/video.
- Has the DMC produced other events at the venue(s) it is proposing?
- Are all expenses (e.g., electricity) included in the proposal?

MAKE YOUR DECISION

Read each proposal thoroughly. If possible, meet with finalists to review their proposals in person. Select the DMC whose proposal most closely meets the needs and objectives of your overall program. Keep all proposal information confidential unless otherwise permitted. Never allow a finalist to read a competitor's proposal.

FOLLOW UP WITH EVALUATION

At the end of your program, ask attendees to evaluate the DMC services. Record the actual numbers of participants on each activity (tours, dine-around, etc.) for use when planning your next program.

If you were pleased with your DMC, ask for suggestions for future programs. Ask them for a listing of their other locations, or recommendations of other companies in cities where you will be planning future programs.

Client Responsibility to a DMC

Since the success of any program is based on communication between client and DMC, it is imperative for the DMC to receive accurate, timely, and concise information. A DMC's proposal should be judged for its depth of information, its ability to forecast challenges and address solutions for those problems, its creativity, its precise costs and its clear verbiage of the DMC's responsibility, so initial interviews should be specific. The client, in turn, should clearly describe the purposes, objectives, and goals of the program and provide a realistic budget. This is discussed more thoroughly in Chapter 2.

It may be a calibrator of the professional planner to seek the services of a DMC, an expert in the field, rather than the planner trying to do what a DMC does best. The result could be the perfect partnership.

The Changing Environment of Destination Management

DMCs will continue to be consultants specializing in trends, fads, and changes. Their role will be that of producer, director, planner, consultant, and strategist.

The forecast will certainly be based on technological factors and the digital revolution. But DMCs must also look at the ideology of the industry, along with the economics and public pulse at a specific moment in time on a specific issue, event, or mood.

THE SURVIVAL KIT

The survival kit for DMCs contains no weapons, rations, or maps. The kit is made up of technology software, ideas, programs, experience, knowledge, customer service, and continued education and certification. The survival strategy should be mapped out. Collective, concerted, and intelligent attention should be given to the map.

For DMCs looking to launch new products and services, the **fast response** trend, a quick operational reaction, will still be the main criterion for success. The successful DMC will take a proactive, rational, and constructive strategic approach.

GLOBAL FORECASTING

A combination of improved communication, international travel, and an increased demand for quality goods and services has created a radical and cresting shift in global business. This movement has not gone unnoticed by the destination management industry. In the infinitely flexible language of the DMC industry, the meaning of the word global partner has emerged. Flexibility, in concert with the client's distinct needs, is the very touchstone of the industry.

How do DMCs marshal the resources, energy, and allies they need? DMCs will continue to partner through consortiums of their peers to exchange methodologies, practices, and standards. These consortiums will no longer have geographic boundaries, but will continue to grow globally. How will DMCs unite to form common standards and terminologies to affect the worldwide industry of destination management? Common standards and terminologies within the DMC industry can only be formed through industry initiatives such as the **APEX Initiative (Accepted Practices Exchange),** sponsored by the **Convention Industry Council (CIC),** whose goals are to develop the best accepted practices for the meeting, convention, and exhibition industries.

DMCs may currently have different approaches to work methods and different words and terminologies to describe services, but ultimately they are all making a contribution to the industry, to their professional field, to their co-workers, even to the world, by making the best use of their talents.

The nature of the global DMC's business has changed. A new understanding of the real potential of the Web, the evolution of the "dot.com" company, and the ability to utilize the tools of e-business have created a more universal, entrepreneurial DMC culture. DMCs will be better equipped to mass-market their own brand of expertise, and, in the process, make their mark in the industry.

Despite the inevitable language barriers, DMCs around the world will still be able to sit around the same tables, talk about the same things, and find solutions.

A SOLUTION: WORKING TOGETHER

Through associations such as IAPCO, ADME, and SITE, the voices of our industry are sounding louder and clearer as the distance and language barriers disappear. When DMCs join hands, they become a recognized force. When that force begins to move, DMCs begin to strengthen their profession through universal education and standardization. Collective action is the first step toward unity.

Technology has changed. People have changed. Ideas have changed. The global age of Destination Management is born.

Key Ideas

"A destination management company is a professional services company, possessing extensive local knowledge, expertise, and resources, specializing in the design and implementation of events, activities, tours, transportation, and program logistics." These companies are responsible for program logistics and program concept. Once client needs have been assessed and verified and the concept established, DMCs proceed to plan the program.

A Professional Conference Organizer (PCO) is the international equivalent of a DMC. The International Association of Professional Congress Organizers (IAPCO) and the Association of Destination Management Executives are two associations that endeavor to increase the professionalism and effectiveness of the destination management industry.

A DMC should be evaluated by a client based on its longevity, financial stability, and client references, as well as its professionalism, basic company structure, and use of technology. The client, in turn, has certain responsibilities to the DMC.

DMCs will continue to be consultants specializing in trends, fads, and changes as the world continues to move toward a global economy. Consortiums of global DMCs and movements toward standardization through initiatives like APEX will aid in this globalization.

Key Questions

1. What is the role of the destination management company?
2. How does a DMC interact with a planner or other client?
3. How do you evaluate and select a DMC?
4. The process of destination management involves many complex steps. How do you use these steps to develop a hypothetical program?
5. How do you see DMCs changing in the future?

Key Terms

APEX Initiative (Accepted Practices Exchange)
Association of Destination Management Executives (ADME)
Certified Meeting Professional (CMP)
Certified Special Event Professional (CSEP)
consortiums
Convention Industry Council (CIC)
Destination Management Certified Professional (DMCP)
Destination Management Company (DMC)
Dun & Bradstreet rating
fast response
ground operators
ground transfers
incentive travel programs
International Association of Professional Congress Organizers
(IAPCO)
logistics
Professional Conference Organizer (PCO)

CHAPTER 2

Program Planning

"After over 25 years spent in the meetings industry, including 22 years devoted to destination management, I am convinced that taking the time to do proper planning will, in the long-run, save time, money, and energy, and will help to ensure a most successful program of well thought out and professionally executed activities."

ILENE B. REINHART, DMCP, CMP

PRESIDENT

ACCESS CALIFORNIA

IN THIS CHAPTER YOU WILL LEARN HOW TO:

- Find qualified clients and have them find you.
- Work with clients to determine program goals and objectives.
- Research demographics of target audience.
- Develop a program proposal that integrates the meeting needs and objectives.
- Bring the program from concept to contract.
- Properly prepare and utilize a schedule of services.

Finding Qualified Clients

A DMC's repertoire of clients includes those from associations, corporations, incentive companies, and social markets, just to name a few. But one does not simply furnish an office and hang out a DMC shingle expecting prospective customers to start lining up. It takes much more than that.

A DMC should join its local **Convention and Visitors Bureau (CVB)** or chamber of commerce and become acquainted with its own business community who may be able to refer business its way. Most CVBs will publish a convention digest that lists up-coming meetings, including the client contact information. A DMC can use this as a good source for mining prospective clients.

Teaming up with the sales representatives of the local hotels to persuade prospective clients that your destination and their property is the perfect place to hold a meeting is a great way to meet with clients at the beginning stage of the planning process. Further work with the local CVBs and hotels by providing services for **familiarization (FAM) trips**—programs designed to acquaint participants with a destination and encourage the booking of programs—will provide a great opportunity to show your company's capabilities through actions rather than just words.

A DMC should narrow down the market it wants to pursue rather than try to spread itself too thin over too many segments of potential client markets. In other words, the DMC might choose to become an expert in serving the needs of the incentive market, and that can be vastly different from the needs of associations. (See Figure 2-1 for a breakdown of DMC market niches.) Once the market niche has been selected, it is important for the DMC to become active through industry associations that provide a forum for networking that can bring the DMC in closer contact with prospective clients.

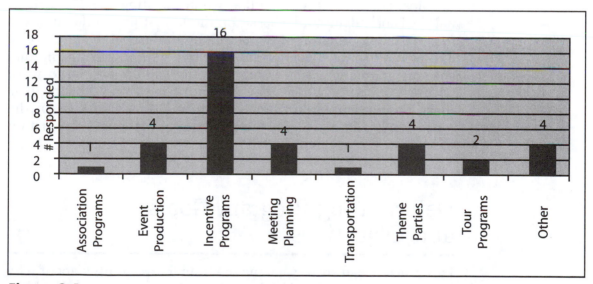

Figure 2-1
ADME DMC Survey—Company Niche
Courtesy of the Association of Destination Management Executives

A DMC should also become an active member of its own industry association, the Association of Destination Management Executives (ADME). Through ADME, one will have the opportunity to meet owners and employees of domestic and international DMCs. This provides the opportunity for personal referrals and introductions to clients from DMCs with whom you have forged relationships. In addition, DMCs can share mutual clients that bring their meetings to a multitude of destinations.

Once a DMC learns about a potential piece of business that may be coming its way, it should do a fair amount of "spade" work to dig for additional information about the lead in order to determine if it is qualified and it if fits within the DMC's company guidelines of what is considered to be a good piece of business. This research should include finding out as much about the company or association as possible, perhaps by reading the information provided on its Web site. If it is an association, find out where it has met before, look up past programs, and contact DMCs that it might have worked with in the past to see what the potential for DMC services might be, especially as it relates to the type of services that your DMC specializes in, such as transportation systems or large-event production.

Most clients will tell you that when selecting a DMC, their final decision might not be based on the lowest price offered or the most dazzling proposal presentation, but rather, on whom it trusts and would feel most comfortable working with toward the mutual goal of producing a successful program. Clients choose to work with a DMC with whom they can cultivate a relationship. It is these relationships, developed over time, that will sustain the long-term health of a highly qualified and professional destination management company.

Determining Program Goals and Objectives

In our fast-paced society, taking the time to really think about why a meeting or event should take place and what elements should be included might seem like a waste of time. "We've always offered tours," or, "We always end our convention with a gala evening dinner," should not be the reasons to perpetuate what might be a bad investment of time and money. Taking the opportunity to delve into what the goals and objectives of the program are and then developing an array of educational opportunities, meetings, recreational programs, and special events that support those measurable guidelines will provide the planner with proven success. It should be the primary focus of every DMC to assist its clients in achieving their stated mission.

First we need to define what is meant by goals and objectives. According to *Webster's Revised Unabridged Dictionary,* © 1998, a **goal** is defined as "The final purpose or aim; the end to which a design tends, or which a person aims to reach or attain." Another definition found in *The American Heritage® Dictionary of the English Language* (4th ed.), © 2000, states, "The purpose toward which an endeavor is directed; an objective." The definition of **objectives** found in PCMA's *Educational Foundation Professional Meeting Management* (3rd ed.), © 1996, is "formalized statements of outcomes to be anticipated as a result of the educational process."

You can see why some planners have shunned the exercise of stating their meeting goals and objectives—a daunting task when looking at these definitions. However, most seasoned meeting and event professionals currently go through this process to help them determine their ROI, or return on investment, especially when the company, association, or organization's management evaluates their budgets and makes decisions as to where program dollars are to be spent.

An example of a meeting goal might be: *To educate the company sales force on new products being introduced to the marketplace.* From that, the next step would be to set well-defined, measurable objectives that, when they are accomplished, will give you the ability to determine that the established goal or goals have been reached. When specifying objectives, the acronym **SMART** will help you determine if they are written in such a way that you will know that the goal has been achieved:

Objectives need to be **S**PECIFIC.
Objectives need to be **M**EASURABLE.
Objectives need to be **A**TTAINABLE.
Objectives need to be **R**ELEVANT.
Objectives need to be **T**IMELY.

Using this SMART guideline, let's set some objectives for the above-stated goal:

By attending the company sales meeting, the sales force will:

- Learn four new sales techniques to use when introducing the new product to customers in the next 60 days.
- Pass a 50-question Web-based examination about the new product within 10 days of the completion of the meeting.
- Integrate the new software, prior to departing the meeting, that is designed to assist in the selling of the new product.

From this exercise, the DMC can provide value-added service to the meeting or event planner by asking explicit questions that will help them target the right set of suggested activities that will meet their meeting or event objectives and goal.

Researching Group and Program Demographics

A valuable step for the DMC is to find out as much about the **demographics** (information such as age, income, gender) of the target audience and the past meetings history as possible by asking the client several key questions. See Figure 2-2 for a list of sample questions. Once these questions have been answered, the responses will serve as a catalyst for the DMC to begin the research and develop a proposal that includes elements that will support the client's meeting objectives and goal.

As an example, going back to the previously defined goal and objectives, the client has answered that the average age of the attendee is 35 and that high-energy, interactive activities have always worked well. In this case, suggesting a new product educational session patterned after a game show format, with interactive capability and instant responses displayed on large plasma screens, might not only be appealing to the client and the attendees, but would reinforce the objective of having the attendees pass an examination about the new product being introduced.

What is the average age of the group?
What is the ratio of the group in terms of male vs. female?
Where does the group come from? Is it a domestic or international group?
Will guests or spouses be attending?
Where has the group met before?
What activities have been done in the past? Of these activities, what has worked and what hasn't worked? If they didn't work, why?
Have these attendees met as a group before?
What are the interests and expectations of the audience?
What budgetary guidelines need to be followed? What has been spent on the activity or activities in the past?
What is the entire preliminary program schedule?

Figure 2-2
Pre-Program Questions for the Client

Program Proposal Development

It is important to know whether the entity asking for proposals is definitely going to be doing business with the DMC or if the DMC is in a bid situation. The answer to this very important question may steer the DMC to prepare a proposal in a variety of ways. The DMC segment of the hospitality industry can be quite competitive, depending on the destination of the meeting. There are some locations with only one or two DMCs; in other areas, there might be as many as 30 to 40 businesses that identify themselves as a DMC. Finding out which companies will be bidding on the project will help the DMC formulate its most competitive strategies for winning the business.

If the DMC is bidding on the business, it will, of course, try to put its best foot forward and not only attempt to sell the program suggestions but also the capability of its company to produce any proposed activities. However, sometimes the DMC might want to proceed cautiously. Not everyone is ethical, and sometimes unscrupulous clients will take the DMC's proposal ideas and present them to another vendor to produce, or will politely tell the DMC that its services are not needed and then will proceed to contact all of the vendors directly and cut the DMC out of the picture entirely. A DMC should be recognized for the valuable contribution it provides to the overall success of a program by serving as the architect and general contractor of the activities that it suggests, not just a free resource of ideas without compensation for the preliminary work that is done.

In addition, another consideration when preparing a proposal should include what the client wants to see and how it prefers to see it. The DMC needs to ask whether a detailed prospectus is needed or whether conceptual ideas with ballpark budget figures might suffice at this stage of the planning process. The answer to this basic question can save a lot of time and energy if the DMC knows in advance what the client expects to receive and can plan accordingly.

On the other hand, DMCs often have the opportunity to work with clients on an on-going basis and may even have preferred, often exclusive, contractual relationships with certain customers that have been developed over many years of working together. For those clients, the DMC will be well informed as to the style of the planner and how clients prefer to receive their information (e.g., extremely detailed with numerous photos and renderings, all e-mailed in a specific format, outlines). Once all of that has been established, the process of developing the proposal can begin.

Let's go back to the game show scenario previously discussed. There are many steps that the DMC will go through to create the type of bid that will "wow" the client and have the client buy into the program concept.

The first step is to develop an outline or treatment of what the end results will look like. Believe it or not, it helps to close your eyes and imagine what you see as the final product. Next, take that visual image and dissect it even further into smaller elements or components. For this example, there needs to be a venue that can accommodate the size of the audience and properly hold the audiovisual support needed for the game show and audience response equipment. The area needs to be darkened to have the audience able to see the plasma screens. The seating seen in the vision might be theater style or even round tables set up with seats set at one-half of the table facing the screen, for example.

From that, the DMC will make a checklist of whom it will need to contact to fulfill the elements needed. In speaking with these vendors, the DMC is putting together a team of professionals where, as the producer, it will guide the vendors through to a successful event. In working with these vendors, the DMC, on behalf of the client, will request the best pricing possible at the most reasonable terms.

Once all of the information needed has been gathered, the DMC will then write a **proposal** that will include a detailed description of the game show that paints a visual picture of what the end product will look like. To support the verbiage, the DMC will often accompany the proposal with graphic images that may include photos of past programs that were similar in nature or renderings that support the descriptions given. In addition, a detailed proposal should include a listing of all of the program elements, a suggested timeline of the event, minimum guarantees, maximum capacities, specific pricing or budgetary guidelines, and optional enhancements that can be considered.

Finalize Program Elements

After the proposal has been presented, it is up to the DMC to follow up with the client to see whether the client is pleased with the proposal or whether any revisions are needed. At this juncture, one very basic decision needs to be made. The client must determine whether it will award its business to the DMC that has presented the proposal that best fits its needs and captured its interest, *even if that means that not all of the final details have been secured.* Any DMC will tell you that one of the most frustrating steps in the proposal process is providing endless revisions before the client will sign on the dotted line. But, when it comes to the point where linen colors are being discussed or the third list of hors d'oeuvre offerings has been presented, that is the time when a client needs to commit.

At that point, the DMC and client should sign a **contract** agreeing to the terms. The program should then be turned over to the program management team to bring to fruition. If the client absolutely refuses to sign a full contract before every detail is in place, the DMC might consider offering a **letter of intent,** a legal document that simply states that the client intends to do business with the DMC for this particular program. A full contract with all the details can then be submitted when all arrangements are finalized. See Appendix 1 for a sample letter of intent.

Discussions within the destination management industry have been going on for many years as to the possibility of charging potential clients for proposal research and development. An enormous amount of time is put into proposal preparation, depending on many factors—including the complexity of the activity or whether the program is something that hasn't been done before, as opposed to something that is *turn-key*. Some DMCs charge for proposal preparation but then offer a credit for this charge if the client contracts with them. Other DMCs will prepare a proposal on a complimentary basis but might charge a fee for subsequent revisions. Of course, these fees are based on many mitigating circumstances, but planners should be forewarned that this is a trend that might become a standard in the very near future.

But let's get back to our example. The game show proposal has been approved and the client is enthusiastically accepting the ideas that have been presented, with just a few adjustments that need to be made. The final sales step will be the drawing up of a legal contract outlining numerous elements including dates of operation, projected program dollar totals, deposit amounts, schedules of payments, and terms and conditions.

A DMC should always seek the advice and counsel of an attorney when developing its general contract format and language, especially as it applies to prevailing laws in its geographic area. From this "shell," all future contract specifics can be inserted. This standard contract may not be accepted as written by every client, but it will serve as a good starting point for adjustments and refinements to make it acceptable to all parties. At no time should a program proceed to confirmation with vendors without a signed contract from a client, including acceptance of financial responsibility for the services that will be provided for them. See Appendix 2 for a sample contract.

After the Contract Is Signed

With the program now contracted, the program management team can proceed with the steps in fulfilling the obligations of the service agreement. The other chapters in this book will serve as the guideline for these steps and will also provide more detailed information as it pertains to budget preparation, vendor relationships, technology, and other elements needed to take the journey down the path toward a successful program.

Finally, all destination management programs should have one element in common. Whether you are in charge of meetings, events, and transportation for a citywide convention for 15,000 or supplying a step-on guide for a tour, all programs should utilize a schedule of services.

At the 2001 ADME Annual Meeting, **schedule of services** (or SOS) was adopted as the accepted term to be used for the "pre-program information distributed to tour guides and field representatives regarding their program assignments." Prior to this, there was no widely recognized name for this document and it was referred to as many things, including trip sheets, staff or work itineraries, itinerary, field staff overview, program timeline, job instructions, production resumes, and function sheets, just to name a few.

The SOS can be further defined as a detailed description of the staff assignment requirements for a given element of a program. The information described on the SOS should provide the staff representative with all of the data needed to perform his or her duties. Ideally, the SOS should be forwarded to the representative in advance of the assignment so that it can be studied and understood prior to arrival on site. The SOS should minimally include the information in Figure 2-3.

In most cases, the DMC staff person responsible for the operation of the program is responsible for the creation and distribution of the SOS. As a check-and-balance system, it is good practice for another DMC staff person to review the SOS for accuracy before distribution.

The timeline for distribution of the SOS varies from two weeks prior to the program to on site, and is mostly dependent upon when the information to complete the SOS becomes available. Understandably, the more time that a field representative has to review and understand the assignment, the better the chances are that his or her duties will be performed correctly.

Within the DMC structure, it is wise to make sure that copies of the SOS are also distributed to the program sales or account executive and to the senior member of the program management

Name of group. This should be detailed to also include any third-party entities (i.e., incentive companies) along with the end user name. Information about who the attendees are is also of great importance so that the representative has a better understanding of the audience they will be serving.

Date and time of assignment

Location of assignment. For instance, do they report to the convention center, hotel, venue, airport or other pre-determined location?

DMC contact names and numbers. This would include office number, cell phone number, home phone numbers, etc.

Vendor information. Include contact name, addresses and phone numbers. Emergency or alternate contact information should also be included should the primary vendor contact be unavailable. An example would be to get the cell phone or pager number of the solo harpist hired through an entertainment agent.

Expected number of guests and venue guarantee numbers. This should also include the number of guest seating that has been provided especially if it differs from the guarantee.

Uniform information. Any special clothing requirements. Example: black pants and client-provided polo (pick up onsite).

Program or account number. DMC's internal reference code.

Detailed program itinerary. This gives the staff person a great overview of the entire assignment even if their duties only relate to a portion of the program.

Vehicle confirmation numbers. These should be requested in the week prior to the program and may be necessary if you must contact the transportation company while on site.

Inventory information. This is pertinent especially as it relates to rental items such as linens or centerpieces.

Gratuity information and receipts. Indicate gratuities already paid, those that will be paid onsite, amount, and those that will be added to the final payment to vendor.

Required permits. Attach copies of street permits, etc.

Routing information and maps. Attach to the SOS.

Menus. Attach to the SOS.

Figure 2-3
Information for the Schedule of Services

team. A valuable method to use is to make sure that a copy of the SOS is placed in a prominent place in the office, such as a common bulletin board or a notebook at the receptionist's desk. That way, should any questions arise, any member of the DMC staff should be able to be of assistance. See Appendix 3 for two sample SOS.

In addition to those already listed, the complete SOS, or perhaps an edited version, is a powerful communication tool for vendors and clients. Because it includes the detailed elements of a program, vendors and clients can use the SOS to review that the confirmed arrangements agree with what was contracted and with what is expected.

In conclusion, communication is the key to any successful program. A DMC wants to ensure the success of a program especially as it relates to their field staff representatives. An important tool to achieving that goal is the schedule of services (SOS) that communicates to the field representative and other interested parties all of the key information they will need to fully perform their duties.

Key Ideas

An organized chronology of events needs to occur before a DMC actually begins work on behalf of a client. First, the DMC needs to find the clients or the client needs to find a qualified DMC. Next, the DMC must work with a client to quantify the goals and objectives of a program or, at the very least, of the element or elements of the program that the client desires.

The DMC must further research the development of a demographic profile of the meeting or event attendees. That information, combined with the defined goals and objectives, can pave the road to the development of a proposal or series of proposals that will meet the measurable standards set forth.

Once a program has been determined, a fully executed contract is drawn that confirms the itinerary of services to be performed by the DMC on behalf of its client. A schedule of services should be created and distributed to detail the responsibilities of the various staff and vendors involved in the program and provides important contact information.

Key Questions

1. Other than joining industry associations, what ways might a DMC search for clients?
2. If there is a short lead time between receiving a request for a proposal and the deadline for the proposal presentation, how should the proposal preparation be organized?
3. What additional demographical questions should be asked of the client beyond those listed in this chapter?
4. What action steps can be taken to have a client commit to accepting your proposal?
5. Other than those points listed, what other pieces of information might be included in the SOS?
6. How might technology help with the dissemination of the SOS in the future?
7. What might be the positive and negative aspects of sharing the SOS with vendors and clients?

Key Terms

contract
Convention and Visitors
   Bureau (CVB)
demographics
FAM (Familiarization) Trip
goal

letter of intent
objective
proposal
schedule of services
SMART

CHAPTER 3

Transportation Services

"Of the seemingly one to two million things that we do to prepare and deliver a quality conference, the 'glue' that holds the enterprise together is the all-important transportation and staffing services of a DMC. It never ceases to amaze me that after all is said and done and we have spent a lot of money, the key to our success is getting our people, whether it's 50 or 5,000, to the right place at the right time, and better yet, making them happy."

DAVID PIERCE, CLU, ChFC, CLF, MSM
VICE PRESIDENT, COMMUNICATIONS & MARKETING SUPPORT
AMERICAN GENERAL LIFE & ACCIDENT INSURANCE COMPANY

IN THIS CHAPTER YOU WILL LEARN HOW TO:

- Recognize that many different types of transportation services are available within the destination management industry.
- Develop and manage the motorcoach shuttle system.
- Prepare a transportation proposal.
- Develop a transportation contract.
- Understand the impact of the Americans with Disabilities Act of 1990 on destination management.

DMCs provide transportation services primarily to their core markets: associations, corporations, and incentive companies.

Planners require many different types of transportation services when bringing their associations, corporations, or incentive program winners to a destination. These services include, but are not limited to, VIP service, airport transfers, and shuttle service (convention and event).

A logistically sound transportation system is a good starting point for an event or convention. Programs organized around safe and timely transportation ensure that all phases of the program are balanced, the guests are moved to the correct location, and everyone enjoys the program.

The event or convention begins the moment a guest steps off the airplane. The program may be doomed from the start if the guests are not greeted by a friendly, helpful person and transported to their hotel or event in a timely manner. If the transportation is synchronized and provided obsequiously by friendly and professional personnel from start to finish, you have just added a special touch to your program, which will long be remembered.

VIP Services

VIP stands for *very important people.* They can range from company CEOs to rock stars to brides. VIPs are treated differently than other people, and their transportation needs and treatment are often enhanced to reflect their status. **VIP service** is a system of providing special assistance to these important guests.

Many corporations, celebrities, and sports figures own their own private aircraft. Flight arrangements are handled differently, and secondary airfields are often used for arrivals and departures as opposed to commercial airports. Ground transportation and meet/greet services differ with these types of arrangements. DMCs need unique information to permit them to greet VIPs with private transportation. Communication is the key to successful VIP transfers. Type of aircraft, tail number, number of travelers, VIP names, telephone and cell numbers, VIP's assistant's contact numbers, and appropriate signage are necessary considerations. Each airport also has its own set of rules and procedures, and during heightened security times, procedures must be verified.

Corporations, organizations, entertainers, incentive groups, sports teams, and so on may also utilize **private air charters** provided by charter companies who lease the planes per trip. A private charter allows travelers to fly on their own terms and on their own schedules. The prices for chartering a private jet vary, depending on the number of passengers and the type of aircraft, catering, and other luxuries that are selected. Ground transportation arrangements for private charters are also handled differently.

When arriving at an airport, VIP personnel are usually greeted in baggage claim. The greeter carries luggage and escorts the VIP to a sedan or limousine. They are usually not required to wait for, or ride with, other guests. Most planners arrange for **standby vehicles** (sedans or limousines) throughout the meeting, event, or convention to ensure the VIP never waits and is on time to all required or desired programs. VIPs usually attend an event or convention by request or for the purpose of showing the corporate or association flag. When VIPs complete a speech, finish with the opening remarks, or attend the main part of the event, they usually prefer to depart. At this time, your private stand-by sedan moves in and takes them to their next desired location. A good rule to use for VIP transportation is to plan for the unexpected request and be ready to accommodate.

Airport Transfer Services

Planners often arrange ground transportation through a DMC from the airport to the hotel or convention property in order to ensure their participants arrive in a safe, timely, and efficient manner. Arranging transportation services ahead of time is an excellent way to welcome guests to the event and reduce attendee concerns, stress, and expense when traveling to a new location. Airport transfers have two key components: *meet and greet* and transportation. These components must be professionally executed in order to make that all-important first impression. A well-conducted airport transfer system for arriving participants is an excellent way to get things started. The same considerations apply when arranging return transportation.

AIRPORT ARRIVAL SERVICES

The key to the success of an airport transfer system is the **meet and greet.** The meet and greet staffs' mission is to ensure arriving guests are properly greeted, efficiently linked with their luggage, and transported to their destination. To set the proper tone, meet and greet staff should be courteous and knowledgable of the airport and city where the convention is being held.

The number of Meet & Greet staff depends on the following factors:

- Number and time of arrivals
- Number of guests on each flight
- Client's desires and budget
- Number of arriving flights
- Vehicle rotation and frequency

Figure 3-1
Meet & Greet Staffing Requirements

Depending on the ratio of meet and greet staff to arriving guests, meet and greet can take place in baggage claim or at a designated location in the airport. Depending on the size and complexity of the airport, you should consider having meet and greet staff stationed throughout the complex in order to direct arriving guests to baggage claim and on to their transportation. To be most effective, meet and greet staff should be easily identifiable. This can be accomplished by having the staff wear a specific uniform or color-coded scarf or hat. Staff could also hold a paddle or sign, or a more interesting item such as a balloon. Whatever the identifying factor, meet and greet staff should always be neatly attired and courteous. See Figure 3-1 for a list of factors to help determine meet and greet staffing numbers.

AIRPORT TRANSPORTATION

Once arriving guests have been received and collected, the next critical component is providing safe, convenient, and efficient local transportation. The size of the vehicle, luggage capacity, safety, comfort, and convenience are major considerations. (For tips on what to look for when chartering a bus, see Appendix 4.) The planner's budget will determine the level of comfort and convenience included in the service. Safety should never be sacrificed and always supercedes other factors. (See Appendix 5 for information on bus safety.)

Some items to consider when deciding on comfort and convenience include the age and condition of vehicles, along with the size and passenger capacity. (See Figure 3-2 for average vehicle capacities.) Also consider luggage capacity. Some mid-sized and

---

Vans	Mini Coaches	Motorcoaches
9–11 seats	20–30 seats	47–57 seats

Taxis, town cars, and limousines may also be used and vary in capacity.

The market dictates the size and type of equipment available.

Figure 3-2
Average Equipment Capacities

mini motorcoaches do have the luggage capacity of the 49-passenger motorcoach, but you need to ask the vendor. Will you require an on-board restroom or television/VCR/music capabilities? Is there a preboarding area with seating, if required? Also check on the air conditioning and heating of the preboard area and vehicles.

If guests arrive on the same flight or at the same time (known as a **mass arrival**), there should be little time spent waiting for the motorcoach to depart once it is loaded. However, if guests do not arrive together (known as **scattered arrivals**), a frequency rate for departures must be determined based on the arrival manifest provided by the planner. The **arrival manifest** must include the passengers' name, airline, city of origin, flight number, and arrival time. In some cases, guests will arrive in small numbers or separately and must be grouped with individuals arriving on different flights. This may require them to wait for transportation. It may also require the planner to establish a schedule utilizing different sized vehicles based on different sized groups in order to reduce the time guests spend waiting. For planning purposes, a 20-minute frequency rate is desirable. This allows the staff to locate and collect guests, locate their luggage, group guests according to location, and escort them to the motorcoach.

AIRPORT DEPARTURE SERVICES

At least 24 hours prior to the end of the program, guests should receive a **departure notice** (in their hotel room or during the program) to remind them of the departure schedule. Once the convention or event has ended, outbound or departure services may be provided. Airport departures are essentially the reverse of airport meet and greet services. At this point, attendees should be familiar with the transportation system provided during the program and may or may not require departure staff on site at the hotel(s). If departure staff is not at the hotel, a hotel lobby transportation schedule card should provide information indicating the frequency rate and drop locations at the airport.

In some cases, primarily small groups departing on the same flight, departure staff will gather the guests, assist them when loading luggage and boarding the motorcoach, and ride with them to the airport. Once at the airport, the departure staff assists with transferring the luggage to the airline desk. The staff remains on duty until all guests and luggage are safely within the airport.

Motorcoach Shuttle System

During the convention or event, transportation from the hotels to and from the convention center/event is often provided. The system that transports or shuttles guests to and from the convention hotels to the convention center is called the **motorcoach shuttle system.** Factors that determine the number of motorcoaches and dispatch personnel (dispatchers) required include budget, weather, size of the convention/event, number of guests requiring transportation, number of hotels from which guests will be transported (some hotels may be within walking distance and others dispersed throughout the city), schedule of events, and the desired frequency rate.

The **frequency rate** is the amount of time between motorcoaches on a given route. The frequency rate is set by the planner and subsequently influences the motorcoach requirement. A frequency rate of 15 minutes means that a motorcoach will stop at a given point every 15 minutes to pick up or discharge passengers. Frequency rates are often different during peak and off-peak periods. **Peak periods** are the times the majority of riders will use the system. During peak periods the major concern is expeditiously delivering and returning convention participants to and from the convention center. Peak periods usually occur at the beginning and end of the day. **Off-peak periods** are the times few riders are expected to use the system. Because the system is not under pressure during off-peak periods, the motorcoach requirement can be expected to decrease. To ensure the required frequency rate is maintained, sufficient dispatch personnel should be on hand to monitor and control the flow of motorcoaches.

Schedules are preferred over frequency rates by some planners. A schedule consists of designated times and locations where motorcoaches will pick up and discharge passengers.

DISPATCH PERSONNEL

The dispatch personnel or staff are responsible for ensuring that passengers are directed to the proper **loading/boarding site**. Dispatchers monitor and control the motorcoach frequency rate or schedule. Additionally, dispatchers maintain a passenger count and determine when and which motorcoach drivers will go on break. Dispatchers should be familiar with the city, as they are frequently asked questions regarding availability of taxis, restaurants, and points of interest. In addition to their professional skills, dispatchers and motorcoach drivers are key to the success of the system, as they are the human contact with the convention attendees.

Dispatch personnel are divided into different positions based on the size and scope of the operation. These position titles may vary in description, but the duties remain similar. In most cases, one person will handle multiple duties described under several positions listed.

The **lead dispatcher** is the on-site person responsible for the transportation system's success. All personnel assigned to the system are under the lead dispatcher's direction. Normally, the lead dispatcher is assigned to the command center for management of the shuttle system, including motorcoaches and dispatch staff. The **command center** is the location used to control the convention or event. This could be the motorcoach yard, a designated headquarters location, or the convention center.

The **assistant lead dispatcher** is the on-site staff member second in command of the transportation system. They assist the lead dispatcher and fill in when the lead dispatcher is not on site. Normally the assistant lead dispatcher is assigned to the command center.

Depending on the number of routes and complexity of the transportation system, you may or may not need a **route manager.**

The route manager is responsible for managing the motorcoach flow into, during, and out of the system for an assigned route. They coordinate directly with personnel responsible for managing the numbered routes, ensure that drivers check in/out, and make sure coaches are tagged and that any changes to the plan are seamlessly incorporated. The route manager is the go-to person for any issues or updates concerning their route(s).

The **motorcoach field supervisor** is located at the hotel or venue and is responsible for motorcoaches arriving at or departing from their respective locations. They coordinate directly with the route manager and provide updates and requests for additional motorcoaches on their route. The motorcoach field supervisor is also responsible for the motorcoach captains and human arrows at their location.

The **venue manager** is the person at the venue responsible for all transportation aspects at the location. The venue manager is also responsible for **staging** coaches at the venue in a manner that ensures guests may depart safely and efficiently. Staging includes designating parking locations and breaks/comfort stops for drivers. The venue manager coordinates directly with the route manager and motorcoach field supervisors on issues concerning the flow of motorcoaches to the venue, as well as directing the motorcoach captains and human arrows at their location.

The **motorcoach captain** assists the motorcoach field supervisor or venue manager in the performance of their duties. Motorcoach captains count passengers and are responsible for the safe loading and unloading of guests.

Passengers are directed to the motorcoach boarding locations by a **human arrow.** Human arrows hold signage, greet guests, present an enthusiastic demeanor, give directions, and keep people moving in the right direction. Human arrows are needed for large venues and hotels to ensure guests do not become lost or disoriented.

When a job requires an extensive amount of equipment, an **equipment manager** is employed to issue and maintain accountability of that equipment. The equipment needed may include radios, uniforms, flashlights, extra batteries, signage, umbrellas, meals, equipment bags, traffic cones, stanchions, and measuring devices. The scope of the job will determine the type and amount of equipment required.

The items for which the equipment manager will be responsible also vary according to the venue. For example, at the Convention Center the equipment manager will be accountable for corkboards, tables, chairs, clipboards, paper, pencils, traffic cones, **stanchions,** restroom supplies, megaphones, radios and chargers, flashlights, coat rack, lock, copy machine, snacks, and beverages.

At the event site, the equipment manager will be in charge of traffic cones, stanchions, illumination for stanchions, flashlights with extra batteries, reflective vests, radios with extra batteries, and snack/lunch/dinner arrangements. Radios with extra batteries, notepads, and writing instruments will be needed at the hotel, and parking passes and identification badges are a necessity at all venues.

TRAFFIC AUTHORITIES

In order to ensure that a transportation system operates as smoothly and professionally as possible, it is always wise to coordinate with the local agency responsible for parking and traffic prior to finalizing the planning process. Areas to cover when meeting with traffic authorities include potential and actual construction zones, presence of VIPs or government officials that may impede traffic, other large transportation systems impacting traffic, and curb restrictions that might impede safely loading/unloading passengers.

Airport Transportation Proposal

Through the client interview process and/or their **request for proposal (RFP),** the DMC will need to learn the information included in Figure 3-3. From this information, the DMC presents the proposal including the type and amount of transportation equipment required to move the participants in the time window projected and agreed upon, and the number of uniformed airport and hotel reception staff needed for the period. The proposal should also include the number of two-way radios to be activated or rented, signage for equipment and staff, and Sky Cap porterage and vehi-

The date(s) of arrivals and departures	The time window for arrivals and departures
Acceptable waiting period at airport for participants between flight arrivals	The number of passengers to be moved
The type of equipment to be engaged	Domestic and/or international participation
The areas of the country (countries) the participants are coming from	If Sky Cap porterage is to be included
Security issues if required	Arrival signage information (i.e., group name, meeting room, required logo, individual's name)

Figure 3-3
Information Required to Create a Transportation Proposal

cle driver gratuities. An inclusive cost is most often constructed per person and is based on a minimum number of people to be moved both in and out over a specified period of time.

Transportation Contract

Following acceptance of the proposal, the DMC prepares a contract detailing the services that have been accepted by the client. It should specify the inclusive cost per person based on the minimum number of participants or projected total for usage of vehicles, staff, and equipment. If actual participation exceeds the contracted minimum, it must state that the client will be charged the inclusive per person cost for the overage.

The document also sets forth a deposit schedule, with the dollar amount and date(s) due. Often it is a two-step process: 20 percent upon signing the agreement by a specified date, and up to 70 percent due by a second specified date. The remaining balance, plus charges for any additional services, is billed upon program completion. This provides the DMC with the ability to place appropriate deposits with vendors in order to secure all services. The deposit schedule and percentage(s) may vary from market to market.

The contract should also state that the DMC has the right to re-cost the program based on the arrival and departure manifest provided by the client.

The Preoperation Process—Inbound Transfer

The client must provide the DMC with clear arrival and departure manifests. The arrival manifest should appear as in Figure 3-4.

After a careful review of the **manifest,** the DMC account executive may exercise the right to re-price the service, and if so, provide that information to the client in a timely manner.

The Operations Department will calculate and confirm the needed transportation equipment (capacity and style). Transportation is ordered to arrive 30 minutes prior to the scheduled arrival time and reports **(spots)** 15 minutes in advance. The size and amount of equipment ordered is based on the number of passengers grouped within the acceptable waiting period, as determined by the client. The turnaround time **(turn time),** or the time it takes to get from the airport to the destination and return, is also important when calculating the amount of equipment required and depends on the distance, time of day, and traffic patterns.

Once the transportation equipment is ordered, operations will also group participants for transport within the acceptable waiting period, schedule and confirm the uniformed staff, and prepare staff instructions. Signs for the transportation equipment and hand-

Arrival Date	Time	Flight	Last Name	First Name	Origin
4/5/2004	8:15	AA 753	Caplan	Mary	Philadelphia
4/5/2004	9:17	Delta 889	Jones	Jonathan	New York
4/5/2004	14:02	UA 4332	Smith	Karen	Atlanta
4/6/2004	13:19	AA 998	Cotter	LaVerne	LAX
4/6/2004	13:19	AA 998	Cotter	Dennis	LAX

Figure 3-4
Arrival Manifest Information

held paddles for staff must be generated once the client approves the verbiage. Operations will notify the **airport land operations department** of the dates(s) and times(s) of the transfer(s), the amount of equipment, and any special security requirements. The airport land operations department is typically responsible for any individual, VIP, or group ground transportation to and from a commercial or private airport. Security may involve U.S. or foreign governmental officials for any individuals requiring elevated security status.

In addition, operations must place appropriate deposits with vendors and arrange for petty cash for Skycap and driver gratuities. A confirmation form, in duplicate, including complete and pertinent information is sent to all vendors and staff. The vendors and staff sign and date the form, retain the copy for their file, and return the original to the DMC operations manager.

Each aspect of the program should be reconfirmed by the operations manager just prior to the date of execution.

Arrival Day Operations

All staff need to report to their supervisor at the airport or hotel 30 minutes prior to the arrival of the first incoming passengers. The supervisor distributes and reviews instructions, arrival manifests, log sheets, and signage, assigns radios, and makes Skycap arrangements, if needed.

A **log sheet** can be used to track staff and equipment. The log should include the staff person's name and may include items such as hours worked and equipment issued. Radios must have an identification number to be recorded on the log sheet.

All staff should wear the DMC uniform and a clear name badge. In some cases, the client may require that the staff wear a specific uniform such as a shirt with client company logo. The airport supervisor should contact the land operations department to review the timing of the scheduled equipment and security issues, if any.

The transportation equipment should arrive 30 minutes prior to the first arrival. The transportation coordinator then meets with the vehicle drivers to review their schedule and destination (hotel), and to place signage on the equipment. Federal law states that drivers for hire can be on call for a maximum of 15 hours and behind the wheel for a maximum of 10 hours.

Meet and greet staff holding signs meet arriving passengers in the baggage claim area or other predefined area. The guests are asked to identify and pull their luggage from the conveyor belt. When the group has formed, the staff instructs the transportation coordinator to move the vehicle from the equipment holding area to the approved airport loading zone. If Skycap **porterage** has been included in the contract, the porter moves luggage to the waiting vehicle. Participants are again asked to identify their luggage as the driver places it in the luggage compartment. The names are verified on the manifest and noted in order to keep an accurate account of arrivals. This process also provides information about no-shows. Flights can be delayed or canceled. The passenger may miss a flight, change arrival time, or cancel plans completely. Any of the above will have an effect on the transfer system, and the staff should be prepared to respond accordingly.

The vehicle is dispatched when it is loaded and the transportation company name, vehicle number, time, and number of passengers have been noted on the log sheet. The airport staff should radio the hotel reception personnel to let them know the time of departure and the number of people to expect. The hotel doorman, bell staff, front desk or special check-in desk, and the client are then informed of the pending arrival.

Generally, the client provides bell staff gratuities. Vehicle drivers are given a gratuity for loading and unloading luggage. Skycaps are tipped per bag at the conclusion of their shift. Market conditions and the geographic location dictate the gratuities. To determine the level of gratuities, you should ascertain the common practice in your community.

Vehicles

According to the Department of Transportation, the following vehicle descriptions are regulation.

> **Bus:** any of several types of self-propelled vehicles generally rubber tired, intended for use on city streets, highways, and

bus ways, including but not limited to minibuses, 40- and 30-foot transit buses, articulated buses, double-deck buses, and electric powered trolley buses, used to provide designated or specified public transportation services. Self-propelled, rubber-tired vehicles designed to look like antique or vintage trolleys or streetcars are considered buses. Over-the-road buses, described separately, are not included in this category.

Demand responsive system: any system of transportation individuals, including the provision of designated public transportation service by public entities and the provision of transportation service by private entities, including but not limited to specified public transportation service, which is not a fixed-route system.

Designated public transportation: transportation provided by a public entity (other than public school transportation) by bus, rail, or other conveyance (other than transportation by aircraft or intercity or commuter rail transportation) that provides the general public with general or special service, including charter service, on a regular and continuing basis.

Fixed-route system: a system of transporting individuals (other than by aircraft), including the provision of designated public transportation service by public entities and the provision of transportation service by private entities, including but not limited to specified public transportation service, on which a vehicle is operated along a prescribed route according to a fixed schedule.

Over-the-road bus: a vehicle characterized by an elevated passenger deck located over a baggage compartment.

Specified public transportation: this includes bus, rail, or any other conveyance (other than aircraft) provided by a private entity to the general public, with general or special service (including charter service) on a regular and continuing basis.

Tram: any of several types of motor vehicles consisting of a tractor unit, with or without passenger accommodations, and one or more passenger trailer units, including but not limited to vehicles providing shuttle service to remote parking areas, between hotels and other public accommodations, and between and within amusement parks and other recreation areas.

Americans with Disabilities Act

According to the Centers for Disease Control and Prevention Web site, an estimated 34 to 43 million people in the United States have chronic disabilities. The **Americans with Disabilities Act** of 1990 was enacted to guarantee equal opportunity and access for these individuals, much as equal access is guaranteed to all individuals regardless of race, creed, color, and so on. Destination management companies must be aware of how this legislation affects the industry. Take time to review the excerpts in Appendix 6 and note how they might apply to planning transportation for a client.

It is imperative for DMCs to demonstrate **general intent** efforts in meeting goals of accessibility. General intent refers to the desire and will to act in a certain way. This includes tracking and documenting all research. They must then plan to address the requirements through written and verbal needs requests. Written requests are generally accommodated on any type of registration form in the information data section, typically labeled *special needs.* DMCs should review their company compliance procedures annually and keep informed of this legislation and clarification of the ADA Guidelines. This is a complex law, and implementation is critical.

It is also important for destination management companies to know the basic dimensional tolerances for compliance with the ADA as their client base is diverse and expansive. Servicing the needs of clients is the first and foremost element of program planning and execution. See Appendix 7 for an at-a-glance checklist of ADA regulations.

Finally, while transportation might not be the most fascinating portion of a program, it is often the key element to making the program a success or leading to its failure. A well-run transportation program might well go unnoticed, but a poorly run program will get everyone's attention. Woe to the DMC who fails to have the limousine arrive on time to pick up the company CEO! The better you understand the ideas and processes behind planning a transportation program, the more smoothly the program will run.

Key Ideas

Transportation is a core competency of destination management companies. DMCs are responsible for planning and executing various forms of ground transportation for organizations and corporations including VIP services, airport transfers, shuttle services, and other ground movements. The staffing for such services is integral to the process, and each team member plays a diverse role in transportation execution. The process of transportation planning includes program analysis, proposal, contract, and execution. Knowledge of modes of transportation and state, federal, and local laws is a part of the planning process as well as the work instruction procedure.

Key Questions

1. Discuss the difference between VIP services and standard airport transfer services.
2. Successful and effective meet and greet transportation services should include what elements?
3. What factors should be considered when planning airport transportation?
4. What factors should be considered when planning a motorcoach shuttle system?
5. Explain the relevance of the Americans with Disabilities Act when planning ground transportation.

Key Terms

airport land operations department
Americans with Disabilities Act (ADA)
arrival manifest
assistant lead dispatcher
bus

command center
demand responsive system
departure notice
designated public transportation
equipment manager
fixed-route system

frequency rate
general intent
human arrow
lead dispatcher
loading/boarding site
log sheet
manifest
mass arrival
meet and greet
motorcoach captain
motorcoach field supervisor
motorcoach shuttle system
off-peak periods
over-the-road bus
peak periods

porterage
private air charter
request for proposal (RFP)
route manager
scattered arrivals
schedules
specified public transportation
spots
staging
stanchions
standby vehicles
tram
turn time
venue manager
VIP service

CHAPTER 4

Tours

"In my 15 years of experience producing tours, I have found that the necessity to entertain attendees by showing them the city they are visiting is still as viable today as it was 30 years ago. Guests want to experience the culture, see the attractions, taste the local cuisine, and capture a memory of the city. Tours are surprising, pleasing, revealing, educational, and offer a kaleidoscope of new perspectives. Creating tours creates experiences."

SUSAN GRAY, DMCP

EXECUTIVE VICE-PRESIDENT, DIRECTOR OF TOURS AND TRANSPORTATION

MAC MEETINGS AND EVENTS

ST. LOUIS, MISSOURI

IN THIS CHAPTER YOU WILL LEARN HOW TO:

- Develop the elements of tours.
- Identify appropriate tours.
- Coordinate marketing and branding.
- Create a tour.
- Establish tour registrations.

A **tour** is a planned trip for sightseeing or inspection. Tours can be unique enhancements to meetings, events, or reunions. Meeting and event planners are responsible for scheduling these ancillary activities and must clearly understand and be able to relate objectives to their tour company. Destination management companies' primary expertise is in the tour planning segment of the list of services that they provide. DMCs are logistical experts, by legal definition, of their particular city or area. Not only are they knowledgeable of all city attractions, historical areas, and shopping centers, but they have other relevant information at hand that may affect the success of a tour. For example, DMCs keep abreast of local celebrations, city constructions, street closings and repairs, and any element that may affect movement on the day of the tour. By using their many contacts, city connections, and experience, DMCs are able to give the safest, most cost-effective, and properly planned tour experience.

Selecting Appropriate Tours

DMCs use historical research to determine and suggest appropriate tours for the group. Demographics such as gender, age, income, group interests, and other pertinent details need to be provided by the planner. The extent of the tour offered will also depend on expected attendance, tour time, and the budget. A variety of tours should be provided to offer options of half- and entire-day tours, optional meals, and educational or recreational choices.

Cost of Tours

Tours are typically sponsored by the organization or paid individually by the guest. Whichever is the case, the cost of the tours should be considered. DMCs base their tour fees on transportation cost, guides, admission fees, food and beverages, and any applicable taxes and **gratuity,** or tips. If the DMC is to provide tour registration (electronic, print, on-site), additional fees will be assessed. Most DMCs will price tours on a per-person basis, based on a minimum number of guests.

Marketing and Branding

Organizations identify their products in the marketplace with brand names, symbols, and distinctive means of identification. Choosing how to identify the organization's yield represents a major strategic goal for the group.

Tours offer an opportunity for organizational or sponsor **branding** (symbol or pictorial design that identifies a product). Tour programs may include the group or sponsor name incorporated in the registration material. Tour tickets and signage also deliver branding messages.

There are many new trends in tour **marketing** (the moving of tours from the DMC to the client, including selling, advertising, etc.) and branding. Some of these include showing company or sponsor's videos on the motorcoach, covering the backs of bus seats with logoed covers, bus signage, and even *shrink-wrapping* the motorcoach with organizational logos or messaging.

Types of Tours

CANNED AND CUSTOM TOURS

Most DMCs have an inventory of **canned tours,** or prepackaged tours indicative of their area. These tours may be historic, educational, entertaining, or recreational. Typical tours range from a half-day to a full-day format that may or may not include meals.

Other tours may be custom-designed to fit the group's needs. Many DMCs offer **walking tours** in their repertoire. These tours have guests walk the streets and neighborhoods to better experience the local spirit and culture.

INDUSTRY/TECHNICAL AND INSPECTION TOURS

Industry/technical or **inspection tours** are tours the client arranges to become familiar with facilities that support or are a part of the client's industry. DMCs will provide the transportation. Tours may include corporate headquarters, working plants or factories, research divisions, and so on.

The information needed to facilitate industry tours includes the name, address, and phone number of the facility. A map or precise directions are required because many of these tours are to places unfamiliar to the motorcoach drivers. Determine from the person arranging the tour who will be the onsite contact. This information is necessary so that in case of a change, the motorcoach driver will know from whom to take directions.

It is also necessary to determine the anticipated number of guests in order to obtain the proper-size equipment. Keep in mind that if you are also running a shuttle during the time of the tour, it is important to select a different departure point for the tour, if possible, to avoid guests getting on the wrong bus. To determine the departure time of the tour, you need to determine the distance to the facility so you can advise the client of the transfer time required.

PRE- AND POST-CONVENTION TOURS

Pre- and post-convention tours are optional tours scheduled immediately before or after the convention. These tours are more complex than the local tours. Added responsibilities include choosing a hotel that will meet the clients' needs, selecting which meals to include in the tour package, and making sure the selected meals offer a variety of foods that will enhance the overall tour experience.

These tours will require the use of over-the-road transportation or airline reservations. When figuring the cost of over-the-road transportation, remember to include a gratuity for the driver and escort. If you require airline reservations, add baggage handling at the airport and the fee charged by the travel agency, if applicable. Gratuities are discretionary, not mandated, and can be a percentage of the program or a flat tip. Gifts are typically not appropriate for drivers or escorts.

Unlike a local tour that is usually completed the same day, pre- and post-convention tours require that you assume the responsibility of planning several days. A detailed itinerary, showing time, location, and description of each day and evening event, must be presented to each attendee. In addition, you will often require the services of a local DMC to provide tour ideas and step-on guide service. Be sure to ask for references, and don't hesitate to check them.

It is extremely important to take into account past history of the attendance on these tours in order to avoid overbooking. A **cut-off date,** a designated day when the DMC will end the registration for the group, needs to be set far enough in advance to avoid cancellation penalties. See Appendix 8 for a checklist for pre- and post-convention tours.

OPTIONAL TOURS

Organizations or associations may choose to offer **optional tours.** Optional tours are tours offered at a designated date, time, and price. The attendee pays for optional tours. Often DMCs' clients are requested to assume the responsibility of accepting reservations directly from the attendee, thereby eliminating any financial responsibility between the DMC and the client.

TRAVEL-RELATED TOURS

Travel tours differ from other listed tours, as they are more related to activities of travel for pleasure. These types of tours can be categorized into package tours, all-inclusive tours, and escorted tours.

A **package tour** is a travel tour bundling several distinct elements, such as air travel, rental cars, and a hotel. A package tour distinguishes itself from a tour by virtue of the fact that it combines fewer elements.

All-inclusive tours have one price that covers all listed elements of the package. Escorted tours are simply tours offering an escort's service. **Independent travel** is a custom-made, one-of-a-kind program designed with specific desires and needs.

An **escorted tour** is group travel with expert guides who manage all the details and share fascinating history and insight on every leg of the vacation. These packages typically include air, hotel, motorcoach transportation, numerous meals, and sightseeing.

Air/hotel packages are designed for people who wish to travel independently, without groups or guides, although they do include access to a local host who can answer questions and steer attendees in the right direction. These packages consist of air, hotel, and airport transfers in a single city, such as London or Paris. Extras, such as half-day sightseeing tours, theater tickets, museum passes, and public transportation may also be included.

Tour operators (a company that assembles the various elements of a tour) are able to negotiate low group rates because they deal in high volume and are able to get hotel and transportation for less than it would cost individuals or families.

Tours are classified according to the quality and amenities of the accommodations selected by the tour operator. These types of tours range from six days to a month, or even longer.

Tour operator programs are endorsed programs administered by the American Society of Travel Agents (ASTA), which certifies that a participating travel agency or tour operator meets certain consumer protection standards.

TRAVEL INSURANCE PROGRAMS

For travel-related tours, travel insurance plans should be seriously considered. **Travel insurance** typically covers trip cancellation and interruption, default protection, missed connections, and travel delays (the maximum for delays is usually $200 per day). It also covers baggage and travel documents, baggage delay, medical expenses, emergency medical transport, accidental death and dismemberment, and travel assistance. See Figure 4-1 for information about trip cancellation and interruption.

Trip cancellation and trip interruption insurance usually pay for fortified, nonrefundable, unused payments or deposits if due to any of the following:

- Sickness, injury, or death of the insured, a traveling companion or family member
- Financial default by the airline, cruise line, or tour operator
- Termination of employment of layoff affecting you or your traveling companion
- Weather conditions causing delay or cancellation of travel
- Your home being made uninhabitable by fire, flood, vandalism, burglary, or natural disaster
- Your being subpoenaed, required to serve on jury duty, hijacked, or quarantined
- Being involved in or delayed due to a traffic accident en route to departure
- Military duty (having your leave revoked or being reassigned within 10 days of departure date)
- Being the victim of a felonious assault within 10 days prior to your departure date

---

Figure 4-1
Trip Cancellation and Interruption Insurance
Courtesy of airdeals.com

- Employee timesheet
- Expense report
- Schedule of services
  - Name of client
  - Client contact if applicable
  - Timing/Itinerary
  - Tour route
  - Any checks for payment to attraction

Figure 4-2
Items and Information for the Guide

Professional Support Staff

Professional DMCs staff well-trained, expert **guides** to lead groups on tours. These guides continuously study their area's main attractions and have learned to present interesting and entertaining information in a rote format to capture the attendee's attention. Professional guides are uniformed and well prepared. **Step-on guide service** is one way these professionals are utilized. A local professional guide is hired to *step on* a motorcoach coming from another city to provide a tour of the area. See Figure 4-2 for items and information for the guides.

Creating a Tour

When creating a tour program, a vast amount of information is required to plan a tour most adequately suited to the needs of the group. Ask the client for the demographics of the group. Age and gender can play a large part in determining the best combination for a tour. Take into account past history. What has appealed to the group in the past? Have there been things they did not enjoy? Does the group have any shared interests? Find out numbers from past tours to help determine the number of buses to schedule for the new tours.

Determine with the client the appropriate length for the tour. Should it be a full day, or would a half-day tour be more suitable?

Know the day or days of the week that the client is requesting a tour. Not all attractions are open every day of the week, and some attractions may be seasonal. Establish whether lunch or dinner arrangements are included in the tour. If the tour continues through the normal mealtime and dining arrangements will not be included, you will need to schedule a stop in a location that has a choice of restaurants so that guests can enjoy a meal on their own.

It is important to determine what the tour budget is and who will be absorbing the costs. Does the association or corporation sponsor the tour? Has it been included in a packaged price, or do attendees pay on their own? Also find out if the client knows in advance of any special accommodations needed for guests. The registration form will include space for guests to submit this information, but if the client knows in advance that all attractions must be wheelchair accessible or an interpreter will be needed, it will make planning the tour easier from the outset.

Keeping in mind all the information from the client, it is time to put together the perfect tour. Be sure to highlight those attractions that are unique to your location. Check the availability of prospective attractions for the required dates and put a **tentative hold** on venues where availability is limited. A tentative hold is a temporary reservation pending a definite booking with no penalty for cancellation. Make note of hours of operation and any admission fees. Check on ADA compliance.

Timing of the tour is critical, as you need to have both bus and guide released at the quoted time to avoid additional charges that cannot be passed on to the client. Keep in mind the time needed to load and unload passengers at each attraction. This will affect the overall timing of the tour, as will the various locations within the tour where the guide will be pausing along the route.

The **tour route** is determined by the total time allotted for the tour. Keep in mind the amount of time required at each attraction. This and the timing will help you choose between highways or side streets. Always steer clear of blighted areas and avoid backtracking along the same streets. Provide a tour route for the guide and driver, including the names of streets and indicating a right or left turn. It is often a good idea to get in the car and drive the route yourself before presenting the tour to the client. Even if you know the city like the back of your hand, construction and destruction can wreak havoc on a once-beautiful drive through the city. It is best for you to find this out so you can reroute the tour.

To determine the costing for the tour, add all costs and calculate the amount of profit you want to generate. Tours are typically priced on a per-person basis so divide the total cost by a minimum number of guests per bus. Show the client the minimum number required to conduct the tour and the maximum capacity per bus. If there is a maximum number that can be accommodated on a tour, the client needs to be advised of this, especially if the client is accepting the tour registrations. Cancellation deadlines and cancellation fees should be shown in the body of the contract and the client should be advised of the last date a bus can be added or cancelled.

Tour Registration

ELECTRONIC REGISTRATION

Tour **registration** may be managed by various methods including phone, mail, fax, and online. **Electronic registration** may be set up within the organization with timely reporting to the DMC, or the DMC can manage the online registration through a link to its Web site from the sponsoring organization. See Figure 4-3 for a list of items to include on the registration form. Electronic registration is the most preferred method, as it offers immediate reporting and tracking and enables DMCs to send immediate confirmation to the

- Name of group needs to be at the top of the form that is returned to the DMC
- Where and when tickets may be picked up—tour registration desk hours
- Name of tour
- Cost per person
- Name and address of participant
- Deadline to receive form
- Day and time offered
- Number of tickets required
- Daytime phone number
- Refund policy
- Check payable to:
- Amount enclosed—by check
- Address to mail check to
- Type of credit cards accepted
- Expiration date
- Credit card number
- Authorized signature

Figure 4-3
Items for the Tour Registration Form

- Name of tour
- Day, date, and time of tour
- Location of tour departure
- Price of ticket (optional)

If more than one tour is offered each day, color-coding the tickets is recommended. Numbering the tickets is also helpful in tracking each ticket sold or refunded.

Figure 4-4
Information for Printed Tour Tickets

registrant. Some programs even permit "at-home" tickets through the registrant's own printer. See Figure 4-4 for information to include on tickets.

ON-SITE REGISTRATION

Many tours will often require an **on-site registration** desk. This allows guests to pick up tickets on site, get information about tours, and buy tickets for tours with spaces still available. The client and DMC need to determine in advance if this service will be offered in order to add the cost of a registration desk into the price of a tour or charge it back to the client. See Figure 4-5 for a handy list of items for the on-site registration desk.

In conclusion, a DMC can build a reputation based on the originality and creativity of its tours. It behooves the DMC to discover the specific needs of its client and customize its standard tours to meet those needs. Familiarity with local attractions, an eye for unique opportunities, and a flair for creative writing are all necessary to create tours that will entice clients to sign up. And

- Description of the tour offered
- Receipts
- Phone
- Preordered tickets in alpha order
- Number of tickets per bus to sell on-site
- Notepads, paper clips, signage
- Patience
- Cash
- Credit card machine
- Information about the city
- Additional tickets for sale
- Information about the convention
- Signage

Figure 4-5
Materials for the On-Site Registration Desk

remember, the key to all successful tours is to reconfirm, reconfirm, and reconfirm.

Key Ideas

A tour is a planned trip for sightseeing or inspection. Tours are unique to each city and, if prepared correctly, can become the highlight of the trip. By using their many contacts, city connections, and experience, DMCs are able to give the safest, most cost-effective, and properly planned tour experience. DMCs base their tour fees on transportation cost, guides, admission fees, food and beverages, and any applicable taxes and gratuities.

Tours offer an opportunity for marketing and branding. Canned tours, custom, walking, industry/technical, inspection, and pre- or post-convention tours are just some of the tours planned by a DMC. Travel tours differ from other listed tours as they are more related to activities of travel for pleasure. Registration may also be requested by the client. On-site registration is an additional option.

The knowledge, personality, and training of the guide are essential to the success of a tour. Step-on guide service is one example of how these professionals are utilized.

When planning a tour, no detail should be deemed unimportant; each aspect of the tour should be timed and carefully planned. Consider each group's diversity and focus on their interests, limitation, and budget.

Key Questions

1. What guidelines are necessary in creating a tour?
2. When would a walking tour be considered appropriate?
3. What type of tour would be appropriate for a group of 45 members of a military reunion group, and why would you select the tour?
4. Identify ways that sponsors of tours may showcase their companies.
5. What are the differences between a local tour and a post-convention tour?

Key Terms

air/hotel packages
all-inclusive tour
branding
canned tour
cutoff date
electronic registration
escorted tour
gratuity
guide
independent travel
industry/technical tour
inspection tour
marketing
on-site registration

optional tours
package tour
pre- and post-convention
   tours
registration
step-on guide service
tentative hold
tour
tour operator programs
tour operators
tour route
travel insurance
travel tours
walking tour

CHAPTER 5

Child Care Programs

"At Monumental Life, we live by a motto that says: Respect people. Make money. Have fun. For us, respecting people means respecting our agents' family time and including their spouses and children in our sales incentive programs as often as we possibly can. However, some destinations are more appropriate for children than others. We had more than 600 children with us at Disney World in Florida in 2000, and another 200 at our recent 2002 sales conference in San Diego. They like having their kids along, and seem willing to pay for children to participate in our Camp Monumental programs and fun-filled welcome parties. At Monumental, we subsidize the costs with the parents to hire professional child care companies to run these programs."

MICHAEL KEY, CMP

DIRECTOR—MEETINGS & INCENTIVES

MONUMENTAL LIFE INSURANCE CO.

IN THIS CHAPTER YOU WILL LEARN HOW TO:

- Understand on-site child care programs and their value to the meeting industry.
- Understand the issues involving the increase in the number of children at meetings.
- Choose between options concerning child care programs.
- Evaluate the risks and rewards of offering any on-site child care/children's programs: risk management, limitation liability, and due diligence.
- Understand safety and security issues related to child care.
- Follow the myriad rules and regulations governing child care programs.

A **convention child care program** is any program that is designed to care for the children of convention attendees during a meeting, event, reception, or tradeshow. This program can be produced by using an existing children's program at a hotel or resort property, by soliciting a group of babysitters to care for the children, by hiring a professional convention child care company, or by taking care of the children in-house.

A professional **convention child care company** possesses extensive knowledge, experience, expertise, and the necessary resources to design and implement a complete children's program. The list of services provided by a convention child care company can vary greatly, but should include complete management of all ages of children, coordination of the children's events, registration, support staff, customized tours and **companion programs,** age-appropriate parties, and **teen hospitality suites.** The actual children's services generally include:

- A nurturing environment for infants and toddlers
- Preschool and school-age playtime fun centers
- Action-packed teen lounges
- Tours to "kid-friendly" places
- Magicians, astro jumps, face painters, craft stations, theme parties, character visits, and so on, along with participatory and recreational activities

During planning stages, convention child care companies maintain frequent client contact, offering their creativity and thorough knowledge of children to design a memorable program. Convention child care companies are determined to have higher standards of competence and skills than those companies that provide only babysitting services. See Appendix 9 for a case study of one of the top convention child care companies.

Convention child care companies are current on all appropriate children's programming, and thus are able to be the best contributors to a successful program. According to Lynette Dummer, CMP, manager of Meeting Services for the Division of Convention & Meeting Services at the American Academy of Pediatrics, "Providing excellent child care is a priority . . . and helps ensure our attendees' children are getting the utmost possible care. It allows parents to attend who might not normally have the means to do so."

Increasing Numbers

Since today's guest's profile differs dramatically from what it has been in the past, special attention should be given to the needs of the attendee. More children are traveling with parents to meetings. According to a Travel Industry Association of America survey, 34.2 million people traveled on business 212.9 million times in the year 2000. Seven percent of these trips included children. The reasons for taking children on business trips vary. Parents wishing to combine business trips with vacation find it financially feasible due to the price breaks often associated with a Saturday night stay. Families, many now consisting of dual-career couples with children or single-parent households, may find that traveling with children is preferable to locating reliable long-term child care at home. Of course, many parents simply enjoy traveling with their children. Whatever the dynamics, the increasing number of attendees bringing children to meetings has affected the guest program planning process. It is the planners' responsibility to rise to the changing face of today's convention attendee.

Child Care Options

It is important to understand that one size does not fit all when it comes to child care and children's programs. Programs should accommodate both the meeting and the needs of all the various age groups. For some groups, the most effective solution to child care concerns is to offer a list of babysitting services to parents. For other groups, a hotel service might be best. But after considering these options, many groups feel the best choice for planners, attendees, and their children is to create a customized program to accommodate all of the age groups, the hours, and the interests of the children. A well-run child care program is an asset to any convention program; the reward is happy children and peace of mind for parents.

For example, the National Speakers Association puts a different twist to its annual youth program. The NSA offers a unique youth leadership program geared toward 10- to 16-year-olds during its annual convention.

According to Stacy Tetschner, CAE, executive vice-president of the National Speakers Association,

Since NSA is bringing in member speakers from all over the world, they ask those speakers who typically present to youth audiences to give a presentation at the youth leadership program. Everything is designed around a central theme and the presenters incorporate that theme into what they are presenting. Typically, the program serves approximately 100 youth each year. Programming includes educational and motivational sessions, fun activities, a dinner and dance on the closing night, and a community service project. In 2002, the program took its youth to Give Kids the World *to help with maintenance projects as well as helping to prepare vases for the* Give Kids the World *float in the Rose Parade.*

This unique youth program allows convention attendees, primarily professional speakers, to travel with their entire family rather than spending another series of nights away from home at yet another meeting.

Client Responsibility

Since the success of any program is based on communication between client and child care provider, it is imperative for the child care provider to receive accurate and concise information. Since a convention child care company's proposal should be judged for its depth of information, its ability to forecast challenges and address solutions for those problems, its creativity, its precise costs, and its clear verbiage of the company's responsibility, initial interviews should be specific. The client, in turn, should clearly describe its objectives and provide a realistic budget.

A planner is not required to have a children's program in order to have a meeting. However, a good children's program will enhance any meeting. Hiring a professional company to manage the children's program, rather than putting babysitters in a room, provides peace of mind to parents. Trying to do the job with inexperienced or volunteer staff involves great risk. The child care services are what a convention child care company or hotel on-site child care program does best. The perfect partnership is that of the meeting planner and a professional child care provider.

Risk Management

DUE DILIGENCE: A CHECKLIST TO EVALUATE THE PROGRAM

Qualifying a convention child care program/hotel youth program should involve a comprehensive checklist that includes:

- *Longevity and experience:* Many companies open and close each year. A convention child care company that has served its community over time has shown that its operation has a proven track record. The provider should have experience in the convention marketplace.
- *Reputation:* Ask the convention child care company for a complete list of client references, with particular emphasis on programs most similar to yours.
- *Basic company structure:* The convention child care company must have a sufficient number of trained staff in order to deliver what it promises. Find out how the staff are hired and if background checks are performed. Are managers CPR-trained and certified? Are managers trained in pediatric first aid? How are the caregivers trained?
- *Insurance and risk management:* Assess the convention child care company's insurance. What level of coverage do they provide? What other insurance does the company carry: Workmen's Comp, sexual molestation, and so on? Can you be added as additionally insured?

LICENSING AND BONDING

- *Safety and security measures:* Does the convention child care company have a written policy for safety and security?
- *Technology:* Check the company's Web site. Ask about its use of computer technology—its ability to provide reports for your program in a timely and efficient manner, for instance.

- *Professionalism:* In which professional organizations does the convention child care company maintain memberships? Is it active in ADME, MPI, ISES, SITE, PCMA, or others?

LIMITING LIABILITY

In order to manage the risk for the planner and limit the liability, it is important that a **disclaimer** releasing the organization from any potential liability be drafted. The disclaimer must be signed by a parent or guardian, who should also grant authorization for any necessary emergency medical treatment. The release should also declare the name of the person who has the authority to take custody of the child. In addition, cautionary measures such as numbered wristbands or photo identification should be provided so that staff has visual proof.

AMERICANS WITH DISABILITIES ACT (ADA) GUIDELINES

It is important to list any special needs of a child under ADA Guidelines. The Architectural and Transportation Barriers Compliance Board (Access Board) is proposing to amend the **Americans with Disabilities Act Accessibility Guidelines (ADAAG)**, adding a special application section for children's facilities. The section contains information based on children's dimensions and anthropometrics, dealing with the measurement of the size, weight, and proportions of the body, for newly constructed and altered facilities. The section would ensure that newly constructed and altered children's facilities are readily accessible to, and usable by, children with disabilities.

The Department of Justice proposes to amend its regulations implementing modifications current with ADAAG technical requirements for children's facilities. This amendment applies to Section 15 of Titles II and III and does not broaden the application of ADAAG; it will only apply to those facilities covered by Titles II and III of the ADA. Section 15 generally does not increase the number of accessible rooms required by ADAAG. For example, the number of rooms or toilets required to be accessible by ADAAG is not changed. Rather, where a room is required to be accessible, it is constructed according to children's dimensions and anthropometrics instead of adults' dimensions. The applicable technical requirements of these sections are unchanged. Other ADAAG sections not specifically referenced in Section 15 shall be applied to children's facilities without modification or addition.

State and local laws and codes, as well as best practices, often recognize the need for certain facilities to be constructed according to children's dimensions and anthropometrics rather than adults' needs.

SAFETY AND SECURITY ISSUES

The type of program to be offered will depend on the needs of the group. In every instance, on-site programs must find a location that is safe. Child care licensing agencies recommend a minimum of 35 square feet per child. However, in the convention child care industry the standard has become 50 square feet per child. The location of the center should also be in rooms with both smoke detection and sprinkler devices. It is advised that the location be away from heavily trafficked areas.

A plan for check-in and checkout must be developed to prevent children from leaving without the authorized person or from being separated from the group. Off-property, it is the planner's duty to develop and review safety and security issues for the children.

Research the background of anyone entrusted with child care or guarantee that the child care company has done so. All providers should be certified in infant/child CPR and a background in child care or education is preferable.

STAFF-TO-CHILD RATIOS

Know the **adult staff-to-child ratio.** If using a company specializing in child-care programs, ask about its staff requirements. The staff-to-child ratio varies greatly from company to company, and recommendations differ, dependent on the resource book consulted. The American Academy of Pediatrics proposes staff ratios as defined in Figure 5-1.

According to Diane Lyons, DMCP, president of Accent on Children's Arrangements, one of the top convention child care providers, the following ratios best ensure that every child

Age	Maximum Child:Staff Ratio	Maximum Group Size
Birth–12 months	3:1	6
13–30 months	4:1	8
31–35 months	5:1	10
3-year-olds	7:1	14
4-year-olds	8:1	16
5-year-olds	8:1	16
6–8-year-olds	10:1	20
9–12-year-olds	12:1	24

Figure 5-1
Staff-to-Child Ratios as Recommended by the American
Academy of Pediatrics
Used with permission of American Academy of Pediatrics,
Stepping Stones to Using Caring for Our Children: National
Health and Safety Standards, *Second Edition, 2002*

feels special and receives the attention and security he or she
needs:

- 1 adult staff: 2 infants (age 0–23 months)
- 1 adult staff: 3 toddlers (age 2–4)
- 1 adult staff: 5 school age (age 5–12)
- 1 adult staff: 8 teens (age 13–18)

These ratios aren't mandated but they are much better than state regulations. These ratios were developed to provide a higher quality of
care. Cutting back on ratios can save money, but can be very risky.

In conclusion, a child care program can be the deciding factor
when potential program attendees are debating attending a particular program. A destination management professional should keep
up with the latest demographic trends in order to intelligently advise clients about the benefits of offering a children's program. The
DMC must determine if children's programs are within its realm
of expertise, or if it will outsource such programs to a qualified
provider. In either case, the health and well-being of the youthful
participants and the peace of mind of their parents must be the

driving force behind all decisions. Then the DMC can put its creative juices to work on making the program one that participants will remember long after the program ends.

Key Ideas

A convention child care program is any program that is designed to care for the children of convention attendees during a meeting, tradeshow, or convention. Services provided by a convention child care company should include complete management of all ages of children, coordination of the children's events, registration, support staff, customized tours and companion programs, age-appropriate parties, and teen hospitality suites.

When qualifying a child care/youth program, you should consider the longevity and experience, reputation, basic structure, and insurance of the company being evaluated.

It is imperative for the child care provider to receive accurate information. A disclaimer releasing the organization from any potential liability should also be drafted.

Key Questions

1. List three reasons that the number of children traveling with their parents on business has increased.
2. Qualifying a convention child care program/hotel youth program should involve what steps?
3. A disclaimer should be signed by the parent/guardian of each child involved in the program. What should this disclaimer include, and why?
4. List three safety/security issues, their solution, and the reasoning behind each solution.
5. What are the adult staff-to-child ratios recommended by the National Association for the Education of Young Children for infants, toddlers, and children up to eight years old? How do these ratios compare with those recommended by leading convention child care companies?

Key Terms

adult staff-to-child ratio
Americans with Disabilities
   Act Accessibility
   Guidelines (ADAAG)
companion programs

convention child care
   company
convention child care program
disclaimer
teen hospitality suite

CHAPTER 6

E-Business and Registration

"A Web-powered registration engine is the key for success with both attendees and event sponsors in requiring 24/7 access. Not everyone is proficient with HTML, so you need to find a way to create a professional online presence that offers a consistent look, yet allows sizzle when needed for your events, from announcement to ROI results and everything between!"

JOHN KRAMER

CLIENT SERVICES MANAGER

CUSTOMER EVENTS DIVISION

CATERPILLAR INC.

IN THIS CHAPTER YOU WILL LEARN HOW TO:

- Determine the effect of e-business on the destination management industry.
- Recognize the benefits and risks of e-business.
- Determine business-to-business challenges.
- Understand the applications of e-business to DMCs.
- Identify the difference between reservations, registration, and online registration.

The growth of e-business has been the inevitable result of the convergence of information and "the need to go faster." Electronic business **(e-business)** is targeting customers by collecting and analyzing business information, conducting customer transactions, and maintaining online relationships with customers by means of telecommunications networks. The economy today is based on the Internet and other technologies. Since use of the Web first began in 1993, e-business has become the leading force in the way business is being done.

Business-to-business segments of e-commerce interactions involve professional buyers and sellers. **Business-to-business e-com-**

merce refers to organizational purchase of goods and services to support production of other goods and services for daily company operations or for resale. (B2B is a popular acronym for the business-to-business market). Most people are familiar with business-to-consumer e-commerce through industry giants such as eBay and Amazon.com. These transactions are minimal compared to business-to-business methods that buy and sell services and commodities. By 2003, the growth of business-to-business e-commerce is expected to erupt to an astounding $1.3 trillion, or about 9.4 percent of total U.S. business sales.

The impact on the destination management industry is that DMCs are finding entirely new markets for their products and services. These are markets that, prior to widespread use of the Internet, did not know about or had little access to DMCs. E-business allows organizations to distinguish their company, goods, and services against competitors. To succeed in the e-business market, DMCs must build seamless integrated systems that will blend existing, self-contained customer information and analyze the consolidated data.

Some popular industry e-commerce resources include A2Z, B-there, MPBid, Cvent, EventPoint, Get There, Passkey, Plansoft, SeeUThere, StarCite, ProcurePoint, and many more. The best process for choosing the right e-commerce resource is to analyze your organizational needs, visit vendor Web sites, ask other professionals what they are using and interview various vendors for capabilities and competitive bids.

Benefits of E-Business and B2B Buying and Selling

The advantages of business-to-business buying and selling versus traditional methods include finding new markets and customers who need the advanced technology to adequately serve their needs, providing for cost savings in every area including marketing and production, and most importantly, reducing the time involved in all aspects of business. The direct exchange of information via the Internet in areas such as order fulfillment and customer service has replaced the conventional methods utilized prior to the Technology Revolution.

Risks of E-Business and B2B Buying and Selling

E-business has not provided a flawless panacea to business models. The Internet has decreased the effects of customer loyalty, premium pricing opportunities, and customer retention. There are numerous opportunities for failure if integrated systems become obsolete or are not updated and continuously upgraded. Neglected training on all systems is a major contributor to e-business failure.

Because enterprise customers are less likely to hire and spend money with vendors who do not display e-business initiatives, organizations must increase their e-business development.

Mergers, Acquisitions, and Franchising

Mergers, acquisitions, and DMC franchising are increasing across the e-services landscape. Both niche and global organizations are making these moves for two primary reasons: (1) to expand into other geographic locations and (2) because wireless and technological capabilities allow it. As customer relationships solidify, customer-centric businesses will be able to provide services in different locations from different offices using different personnel. **Customer-centric** is an innovative, market-proven methodology to identify customers' unstated needs and consistently develop products that meet those needs.

E-Business Challenges

Whatever new trends are born from the e-business methods, the key considerations in program fulfillment will remain constant:

- Service needs
- Reliability
- Availability
- Scalability
- Security

- Budgets
- End user customer needs
- Management

What are the e-commerce challenges?

- Enabling a greater return on investment (ROI) and infrastructure investment
- Providing a continuously available infrastructure to support mission-critical application environments
- Hiring and retaining skilled IT and network support
- Gaining access to the latest technologies
- Focusing on core competencies
- Driving down costs
- Supporting an increasingly remote-based work force
- Ensuring brand value
- Increasing concern over cyber security

COMPUTER AND INFORMATION SECURITY

Computer security is one of the fastest-growing professions in the world. As a result, a whole new cadre of technical support experts have emerged, and organizations are forced to understand how computers and networks work. Every user needs to be informed on defensive measures.

Organizations and their employees benefit when they are able to access office networks remotely. With broadband communications, fast data transfer makes remote connectivity practical and productive. With this benefit come risks. If not properly protected, systems can be vulnerable to intrusive attacks. However, with careful planning and implementation of guidelines and best practices, organizations can support the remote usage of systems while protecting their networks and information systems.

Careful attention to security enhancements and utilities of new technology can mitigate any vulnerabilities. Security management and guidelines should address areas of risk management, security management training, and awareness.

There are multiple programs available that are security-oriented. These programs offer computer security, replacement user interface, access control, file protection, user oversight, remote systems administration, and policy management. Programs can also audit trail logging, a record showing who has accessed a computer system and what operations he or she has performed during a given period of time; monitor Web browser usage; require usage authorization; control software distribution; and aid in troubleshooting. They support single sign-on and biometric authentication, the prevention of changes to configuration settings in a machine. Other security products are listed in Figure 6-1. The key to security management is integrating and analyzing data from all of your computer systems. The basic architecture for the management will be query-based correlation, which relies on all the data being pres-ent in a database for later analysis or in-memory techniques where the correlation service processes the inbound information in memory as it arrives.

Ultimately, regarding security management and risk management, awareness of a real-time threat identification solution must be part of your system guidelines.

A professionally trained IT administrator is highly recommended to set up and manage internal computer networks and security.

Desktop antitheft products	Laptop antitheft products	Asset recovery
PC access control products	LCD projector security products	Computer lab antitheft products
Privacy filters and screens	Disk drive locks	Security cables
Security fasteners	Office security	Web access control
Encryption	Antivirus, malicious code, gateway and e-mail security	Proactive Internet policy enforcement
Security appliances and content filtering	Hardware-based software protection	Antipiracy and secure software licensing
Antipiracy software protection	Secure trialware	Software licensing
Electronic software distribution	Electronic software activation	Online purchasing and downloads

Figure 6-1
Security Products

E-BUSINESS LEGAL ISSUES

Legal and practical issues have surfaced with the emergence of e-business. Some of the issues include jurisdiction, privacy, intellectual property infringement and tortious conduct, a wrongful act, or damage for which a civil action can be brought.

When building a Web site, you should first put together a team to design, develop, and host the site. As with any supplier, formal agreements should be signed by all parties agreeing to a development schedule that outlines the timetable for testing the site, establishing ownership and deliverables. The contractual agreement should include all requirements and basic elements that are included in your other business contracts: an offer with definite terms; acceptance of terms; requirements of consideration; statute of frauds; description of services; payment, cancellation, and termination terms; contingency clauses; and any other terms recommended by your attorney. The supplier must obtain rights to the deliverables before the site is created. Also, when writing a Web site hosting agreement between you and your supplier and the supplier's Internet service provider (ISP), you need to decide what type of Internet connection is being used and whether you have the necessary back-up to protect against problems. You must also address the issue of the domain name for the Web site, acquisition fees, and terms of ownership. Once the site is up, you will want to post *terms and conditions* for visitors' use of the site. Terms and conditions are similar to your business contract terms with the exception of language, which will include Internet terms.

Terms to be addressed should include, but not be limited to:

- The right to upload content
- Consent to use information
- Terms and conditions governing the sale of goods and services
- Accept buttons
- Proprietary rights
- Disclaimers of liability and warranty

E-BUSINESS PRIVACY ISSUES

A number of privacy issues apply to e-business and privacy concerns with regard to information provided via a Web site that must be addressed. Currently, privacy policies are not legally required on a Web site. If you choose to put a privacy policy on your site, you might consider registering your privacy policy with an industry self-regulatory organization.

E-Business Application to Destination Management

The future is luminous for destination management companies that take advantage of the monumental potential of e-business. Since the late 1960s, the emphasis on most DMCs has been to run production-oriented operations. These companies have traditionally focused their energies on meeting support services and promoting those services to customers in hopes of selling enough to cover costs and earn profits. They found that creating long-term relationships with customers would pay off through repeat business and better sales.

DMC E-BUSINESS SOLUTION FOR DATABASE MANAGEMENT

Traditionally, sales centered on a one-to-one interaction between a salesperson and the customer. Buyer–seller relationships were easy to manage and easy to track.

E-business has created the need for **database management,** which refers to the use of computers to analyze data and then identify and target specific groups of potential customers. This innovative approach has become an effective tool for building specific groups of potential customers by allowing sellers to sort through large amounts of buyer information to fine-tune target customers. Modern information technology provides essential support for lasting customer relationships. DMCs can track history and buying patterns, develop customer profiles, customize their product and services offerings and sales promotions, reduce errors, invoice and track payments electronically, and personalize customer service.

A properly designed and implemented database improves customer retention and referral rates, boosts sales, and reduces the direct cost of marketing expenditures. Internet connections bring instant feedback from customers. This accessibility and speed helps DMCs respond quickly to changes.

Web sites provide real value to buyers and visitors. They allow information processing and presentation. Web sites backed by databases are indispensable tools for destination management companies. A well-designed Web site and database will provide electronic data interchange, add the ability for national and global account selling, manage inventory, and measure evaluation techniques.

ONLINE RFPS AND PROPOSALS

Contemporary e-business has changed the way that DMCs submit proposals. With the advent and creation of online requests for proposals (RFPs) come the business response of online proposals. Online RFPs are gaining a foothold in service requests from buyers to sellers. The online RFPs typically include the client profile, meeting/event information, venue requirements, food and beverage requirements, special needs, tour requirements, program history, dates of programs, due date for proposal, and—if DMCs are lucky—the budget.

If RFPs are sent online, online responses are advised. Buyers will look for sellers whose electronic environment best matches theirs. Online proposals should provide all necessary responses to requests and should also include any color photos, floor diagrams, and necessary graphics. Hard copies (print) should only be mailed if the client requests that type of format, if print marketing collateral is necessary, or if the client's computer infrastructure does not allow receipt of large electronic files.

METRICS REPORTING

After all programs, meetings, and events are completed, what tools are needed to measure success and turn all reporting efforts into valuable information? By leveraging **data mining** (seeking hidden patterns in a data group that can then be used to predict future behavior) and **metrics reporting,** destination management companies acquire valuable information regarding their sales, customers, on-site operations, measurable outcomes (hotel room pick-ups and no-shows, airline travel, tour and activity participation, etc.), and other relevant information.

Metrics, generally, are the measurable characteristics. In computer application, *metrics* refers to authentication techniques that rely on measurable physical characteristics that can be automatically checked. Metrics reporting plays a critical role in the future of technology, and especially in electronic commerce.

Web metrics reporting tools are custom-designed to meet the organization's needs. In addition to customer activity, data mining organizations are able to determine the most effective actions for their e-business with these tools:

- *Order information:* Organizations can run reports on orders by dollar sales for any time duration.
- *Customer information:* Metrics reports provide organizations with buyer demographics including age, gender, income, geographic information, or any other information that the group wants to collect.
- *Sales data mining:* The sales data mining reports measure the success of particular products in the organization's online solution.

Evaluation of data is critical to measure every aspect of program planning.

Registration

Registration services are part of the common offerings of most destination management companies. **Registration** is defined as adding a name to an official list. Although this appears to be simple and straightforward, certain steps must be taken to ensure accuracy and success in completing this process. Tour, meeting, and housing registration will be examined in this section.

It is assumed that the destination management professional will be using some type of computerized software to accomplish this process. However, any registration can be carried out manually by the use of information cards—usually 3- × 5-inch cards, ledger sheets, and typewritten lists. This was, after all, the proven method prior to computers.

Three components are common to all registration types:

1. Advance planning
2. Implementation
3. Post-event statistical reporting

TOUR REGISTRATION

Advance Planning for Tour Registration

The client and the DMC will have already made the choices of tours based on the accepted proposal. Now they must decide on the following:

- What is the maximum number of spaces available for each tour?
- What is the minimum number required to implement each tour?
- How many **comp spaces**—additional spaces at no charge, or *complimentary*—are there (if any)?
- What is the deadline date for advance registration?
- Who is the **source of information?**—Will the DMC receive information directly from the individuals, or will everything be filtered through the client?
- Who is in charge of payment management (client or DMC)?
- If the DMC is handling payment methods, what will be accepted? Cash, check, money order, wire transfer, credit card, purchase order?
- If monies have been added to the tour fee, what is the schedule of payment remittance to client?
- Will tickets be used, or will attendees be checked off a list? If tickets are used, will they be mailed in advance or picked up on site?
- What confirmation methods will be used? E-mail, fax, or mail?
- What is the cancellation policy?
- Is the tour information accurate? The DMC should sign off on information prior to publication to ensure date, time, and payment accuracy.

Although most of these steps are straightforward, certain components should be emphasized, beginning with the minimum number of spaces required and how tour cancellation will be accomplished should a group become complacent or displeased. The cut-off date comes into play here and should be no less than three (3) weeks prior to implementation. This will allow the registration staff (whether it be DMC or client) to provide individuals the opportunity to switch to another tour or to receive a refund if their original tour is cancelled. The three-week period is vital because many people attending the program during which the tour is offered may leave home a week early to explore the area, for example. This is especially true of those who are attending from other countries. Three weeks is usually sufficient time to contact the respective individual. Although communication time has been lessened with the advent of fax and e-mail, not everyone has access to these methods so they should not be the sole method of communication when canceling an activity.

If the client has chosen to be the source of information, determine what will be supplied to the DMC and in what time frames. In some instances, only raw numbers are given, while in others the actual forms or a list of attendees is supplied. It is important that the client is aware of, and will adhere to, previously scheduled reporting dates so the DMC can give the highest quality of service.

If the DMC is to receive the information directly from the registrant, determine how receipt of information and funds will be confirmed. At the very least, this confirmation should include the name of the group/event, the tour name or identification, and a statement of the amount of payment received. Ideally, it should also include the cancellation policy and directions for reaching the tour departure point. Furthermore, a liability waiver should be included, along with instructions on completing and submitting the waiver if this was not part of the registration form. Blank waivers should also be available at the departure point.

When the DMC is to receive the information and monies directly, it should be decided well in advance what payment types are acceptable. For advance registration, checks and money orders payable in U.S. dollars and drawn on a U.S. bank are recommended if the event is being held in the United States. Non-U.S. programs may also require U.S. funds, depending on what the organizer/client has chosen. (*NOTE:* Individuals from most countries outside the United States can accomplish currency exchange. Sadly, however, it is not so easily accomplished in the United States. Many smaller towns and cities do not have this service available at all, and even larger cities only offer one or two outlets for this service.)

Wire transfer service via fax or Internet should be offered in instances when a considerable percentage of attendees will be coming from other countries. The bank through which this service is offered will usually charge a set fee for each transfer, and this additional fee must be made clear to the organizer/client so the information can be included in the instructions for registration.

Credit-card payments can increase registration for the program because of the ease of using a card. However, the DMC must make provisions to handle the processing charges, which are incurred by allowing the use of credit cards. The fee is a percentage of the payment made, depending on the amount of activity the DMC has through the respective *merchant account.* Further, since some credit-card companies charge a higher percentage than others, the DMC may choose to limit the type of cards that will be accepted.

It is not recommended that tour registrations be accomplished via the **purchase order** (P.O.) method. A purchase order is a *commercial document* used to request that someone supply something in return for payment. Accepting purchase orders requires the DMC to send out an additional mailing to the P.O. issuer and results in a longer waiting period before funds are paid.

The refund policy must be determined and published in advance. Ideally, no refunds will be made on site (there will, of course, be some exceptions based on circumstance) and acceptable requests for refunds received after the registration deadline should not be made until the event is complete. For example, more than three weeks prior to the program, a refund minus the administrative fee can be made. After that deadline, refunds will be made within two weeks following the program. All refund requests should be in writing. Refund policies vary from company to company.

Implementation of Tour Registration

Once the advance planning is complete, registration can begin. The required information should be entered, using registration software or a database program. At the very least, the name of the group, the name (or other designator) of each tour, the dates of each respective tour, and the price should be included in the registration.

The number of spaces available is then assigned to each tour and the registrant's name and fee paid are entered. The program should then reduce the space by the appropriate number of registrants. Some software programs are designed to let the operator know when space is getting low. Confirmations can be e-mailed or printed and mailed to the registrant. There are two schools of thought on mailing the actual tickets. One is that tickets may be lost prior to reaching the meeting, thus creating additional work on-site in replacing documents. The other is that mailing the tickets reduces the wait and length of lines on site. The method for ticket disbursement should be decided in the planning stage.

At the end of the advance registration period, final lists, additional tickets for each tour, and the source documents should be taken to the tour desk in order to facilitate any problem solving. Once the program is completed, additional registrations and any other pertinent data should be entered into the system in order to have a complete report for the client.

Post-event reporting is an important phase of the registration process. It provides a library of archived information for future programs as well as an ROI (return on investment) analysis.

The post-event evaluation reviews revenue generations, cancellation impact, pre-event registrant numbers, on-site registrants, and any other field of information needed to accurately evaluate the registration process.

MEETING AND EVENT REGISTRATION

Advance Planning for Meeting and Event Registration

As stated earlier, many components are the same as for tours and should be settled during the contracting period. The following list is a guideline:

- How many attendees are anticipated?
- Is there a maximum to be accepted?
- What fees, if any, will be charged?
- Who will collect fees (DMC or organizer)?
- Will multiple sessions need to be tracked?
- Are there separate session fees?
- What payment method(s) are to be used?
- Will a toll-free number for registration be required?
- What type reports does client/organizer need? (e.g., financial, chronological, alphabetical, registration types and categories)
- What is the communication/reporting schedule?
- How should information appear on badges?
- What type of badges and badge holders are required?
- Is there more than one badge type (e.g., exhibitors, staff, attendee)?
- Will this require different colors of badge stock?

- Is there ancillary information to be included in registration packets?
- Who will be responsible for securing information and inserting it in packets?
- Who sends confirmation and what information should it contain?

Should there be multiple sessions, separate sessions, or activities with fees, the registration form will need to be designed to make this information stand out clearly for both registrant and processor. Ideally, the processing entity would have an opportunity to review the form in the design stage to ensure clarity.

How information should appear on badges may seem to be an unnecessary question; however, one needs to know, for example, if it is a simple matter of first and last name, or large, centered first name and smaller last name on the second line. If it is an international event being held outside the United States, it is quite likely that there will be titles, such as Mr., Mrs., Miss, or Dr., printed on the badge. Many times, people from non-U.S. countries desire more formality. Business classifications might also be required (e.g., human resources, PTA president, or Northwest District). In any event, the information to be captured and printed may require a programming change.

The type of badges and badge holders used will again be a matter of the client's preference and may even reflect some traditions within the group or organization. Depending on badge dimensions, additional programming might be needed for this as well. It may also be that if there is more than one badge type in different colors, the staff time cost might be affected. This requires dividing printing into different sections in order not to waste badge stock.

Should there be ancillary information included in registration packets, it is important to know who will be responsible for obtaining the material, as well as inserting it. Ideally, the group who is handling the registration management will be responsible for including the material in the packets. (When material is added on site by volunteers, they are unsure as to whether a badge or other products have been run and, conversely, the registration manager is unsure as to whether every person has the information that should have been received.) Although this might slightly raise the cost of the service, it usually pays for itself in achieving a smooth, seamless process on site.

Implementation of Meeting and Event Registration

Confirmation information is generally sent by the registration management service. It is important to know what the confirmation should include. If it is strictly a notice that the funds have been received and a guest is registered for the conference, this could be handled with a form letter. However, in the event of multiple sessions and events, the client/organizer might want each of these components listed, which would require a programming revision.

As was instructed with the tour segment, maintain periodic communication with the client. At the culmination of the advance registration period, all adjustments to categories and monies should be made and reports should be sent to the client. Then it is a matter of organizing the printed products in the manner desired by the client and taking all reports and source documents to the site.

If your company is also managing the on-site component, you must have, or be prepared to give, logistical details such as number of computers and printers on site, hours of registration operation, available space in registration area, number of counters and/or tables needed, who will handle policy decisions that may arise, and refund policy.

Following the meeting, all on-site registrations should be a part of the final report recapping attendance, sessions, and special activities. At the point of contracting, an agreement should be made that clearly states that a portion of the registration fees should be maintained by the registration management company in the event that refunds are to be made by the registration company rather than the organizer. An agreement as to how long these funds will be held is necessary. This could be as long as 90 days. Following the final settlement, any requests for refunds will be forwarded to the client.

Post-event reporting captures historical data that are necessary for the next program planning. The information collected conveys accurate attendance numbers, no-show numbers, activity attendance, and any other reportable information required by the client.

HOUSING REGISTRATION

Advance Planning for Housing Registration

In most instances, the client will have already negotiated and contracted for the hotel rooms required. In this event, the destination management professional and the client need to agree on the following:

- Dates block is being held*
- Total number of rooms*
- Room types (single, double, triple, quad, suites)*
- Number in each room being held each day*
- Room rate by type*
- Cutoff deadline
- Cancellation policies of hotel
- Deposit amounts
- Method of payment (if not paid by client)
- Substitutions and changes

Starred (*) items should be entered into the housing program being utilized. The program should be one that reduces the **room block** each time a reservation is entered. Most importantly, it must be able to capture the name, address, and contact information of the individual registrant. At some point, whether it is by the client, hotel, or DMC, a confirmation or an acknowledgment must be sent to the registrant. Refer to Figure 6-2 for a sample housing registration form used to capture information.

A **fact sheet** should be available to all members of the staff who might possibly have contact with the registrant. This sheet should include the cutoff deadline, hotel cancellation policies, deposit amounts, and methods of payment. Other helpful items could include a description of the hotel and its amenities, the distance from the airport, and available transportation and cost.

The question of substitution and/or cancellation policies should be addressed at the beginning of the program. These two items are important because if no substitution is allowed, the hotel might be able to inform clients that they did not meet their room block commitment, even though there might be registrants waiting for accommodations. In any event, the DMC professional will need to know what type of cancellation fee applies.

Inserting a new name into a room that a previous registrant has canceled is recommended highly over losing the room entirely. However, the client must be aware that some type of fee should apply to cancellations (at least to the housing entity), because canceling reservations expends a lot of time and effort. This is because there can be multiple records to be changed and sent to the hotel, registrant, and client. Additional postage and communication vehicles will have to be factored into the budgeting process.

DMCs traditionally do not handle large groups for housing. If the group is more than 200, usually a third-party housing company

December 2–5, 2004 ▪ The Royal Palm Crowne Plaza ▪ Miami Beach, FL
Conference Registration/Hotel Registration Form

Association of Destination Management Executives
INTERNATIONAL

Register in one of three ways:
By mail: ADME, 3401 Quebec St. #4050, Denver, CO 80207 —*OR*— by Fax-303-394-3450 —*OR*— by Internet: HTTP://www.ADME.org
Please print or type. Registration **DEADLINE:** November 10, 2004.

Mr. Mrs. Ms. Last Name on Passport: First: Mid. Init.

Badge Name: Title:

Company Name:

Mailing Address: Suite #:

City: State: Postal/Zip Code: Province: Country:

Work Phone: Fax: E-mail address:

Registration Fees: *(Fees include education sessions, breaks, lunches, and reception unless otherwise noted.)*

❏ Member fee—$400.00
❏ Staff of Pre-Registered Member—$350.00
❏ Nonmember fee—$480.00   **Registration total $** _____
❏ Staff of Pre-Registered Nonmember—$430.00   *($25.00 per person additional fee assessed after November 10th deadline.)*
(All funds must be in U.S. dollars and drawn on a U.S. Bank. Fees include education sessions, breaks, lunches and reception.)
I authorize ADME, or its Agent, to charge my registration fee(s) to my credit card. I understand the cancellation and other policies stated in the
conference brochure. **All changes or cancellations must be in writing.** *(All funds must be in U.S. dollars and drawn on a U.S. Bank.)*

Optional Programs:
Wednesday, Dec. 1, 2004   **Friday, Dec. 3, 2004**
____ Certification Study Session x $90.00 = _____   ____ Dine A Round   x $ TBD = _____
Thursday, Dec 2, 2004   **Sunday, Dec. 5, 2004**
____ Art Deco Walking Tour   x $25.00 =____ (limit 15)   ____ Art Deco Walking Tour x $25.00 =_____(limit 15)
____ Everglade Tour   x $34.00 = ____ (minimum 20)   ____ Everglade Tour   x $34.00 =_____ (minimum 20)

Tours are non refundable once purchased.   **Optional Program total $**_____

Housing Reservations - Royal Palm Crowne Plaza Resort
Reservation Deadline: November 10, 2004

Arrival Day/Date: _____   Departure Day/Date: _____

_____ Single Room $140.00 + 12.5 % tax.   _____ Double Room $140.00 +12.5 % tax.
An additional Resort Facility fee of $10.00 per room, per day, will be collected by the Resort upon departure .
Call ADME for Suite information: 303 394-3905
Additional occupant name: _____
                    (Reservations are based on Non-Smoking Rooms unless indicated.)
❏ Yes—Smoking Room   ❏ I require special accommodations to fully participate.
                    Explain your needs:_____
A portion of the room rate is used to defray some of the meeting costs.
The Royal Palm Crowne Plaza Resort requires a valid credit card number to guarantee your room reservations.
Payment type:
Credit Card: _____   Exp. Date _____

(Please see brochure for guarantee policy.)

Registration total $_____ + **Optional program total $**_____ = **Grand total $**_____
($25.00 per person additional fee assessed after November 10th, deadline.)
Payment type: ❏ Visa   ❏ MasterCard   ❏ American Express   ❏ Check (payable to ADME)
Credit Card #: _____ Exp. Date: _____
Billing Address:_____
Signature: _____

2002—Miami Beach

Figure 6-2
Sample Registration Form Including Housing
*Courtesy of the Association of Destination Management
Executives*

or city housing bureau is used. The groups handled by DMCs are typically VIPs or closely held incentive groups to which the client wants special attention given.

There are off-the-shelf housing programs on the market, but using them will require some study and practice time. A DMC may also choose to develop its own housing program using a database-driven spreadsheet. That, too, will require time and practice.

Implementation of an internal housing program can vary from a basic database format utilizing limited information fields such as name, company, title, address, telephone, e-mail address, preferred hotel, room request, special needs, and so forth to a more complicated format including many fields of information that a client might want to capture for customer insight (sales forwarding and follow-up). You will use your housing list to monitor sleep room requests. Other information that will need to be provided to attendees includes:

- Name and address of the organization
- Contact information
- Billing instructions
- Reservation deposits
- Cutoff dates (last day to register)

The hotel will process the reservations once they receive the housing list.

Post-reporting analysis provides a final report showing the actual number of rooms used, the total number of rooms originally blocked at each hotel each night, how many of these rooms were sold and unsold nightly, and a summary for all hotels showing total room nights sold and unsold.

THE EFFECT OF E-BUSINESS ON REGISTRATION

Most successful DMCs use one or more types of online registration. With large programs and daily workloads, it makes sense to offer electronic registration. DMCs spend hours organizing invitations, flight manifests, housing reservations, meeting and delegate registrations, tour registrations, and event reservations. E-business solutions for registration enable DMCs to offer the following:

- Registration process engineering
- Web site linking for registration
- Registration form design

- Data entry
- Internet Web site registration hosting
- Confirmation mailing
- Badge production and mailing
- Event attendance tracking
- Tour attendance tracking
- Security monitoring

Utilizing automated registration services also allows DMCs to provide custom interactive lead retrieval, which can increase attendance and automate the sales follow-up process. Online registration saves money and time, and makes the registration process more simple.

Destination management companies can still offer personnel assistance for registration, including registration supervisors, network technicians, and data entry support staff. Other capabilities include fulfillment of badge stock, badge holders, ribbons, lanyards, confirmation postcards, custom mailing pieces, and promotional specialties.

Organizations providing any type of registration support should also provide registrants with options for fax services, stuffing and mailing inserts, 1-800 service for U.S. and Canadian registrants, secure credit-card processing, daily financial reporting, on-site hardware and software, registration booth requirements, and any required sales lead materials.

In conclusion, e-business has revolutionized the way business is done, and the field of destination management is no exception. From buying and selling, to registration and invoicing, technology has allowed companies to save time and money while strengthening their product or service. It is essential for today's DMCs to understand and utilize the benefits of e-business to stay competitive and avoid being left in the cyber-dust.

Key Ideas

Dramatic changes in business methods and electronic commerce have revolutionized the destination management industry. E-business has turned virtual reality into industry reality through computer and communications technology. Business-to-business (B2B) buying and selling has opened up new markets for DMCs, but decreased the effects of customer loyalty, premium pricing opportunities, and customer retention.

E-business has created the need for proper database management, creative Web site development, and the innovative use of technology for items such as online proposals and RFP responses.

Registration is defined as adding a name to an official list. Tour, meeting, and housing registration each offer different challenges and solutions, but three components common to all registration types are advance planning, implementation, and post-event statistical reporting. Online registration is here to stay and offers many benefits to both DMC and client, not the least of which is the time savings involved.

Key Questions

1. Define and differentiate between e-business and business-to-business.
2. Provide two benefits and two risks of e-commerce.
3. List five e-commerce challenges that face destination management companies.
4. How are DMCs using e-commerce to manage their business?
5. What is the difference between cancellation and substitution?

Key Terms

business-to-business e-commerce	fact sheet
comp spaces	metrics reporting
customer-centric	purchase order
database management	registration
data mining	room block
e-business	source of information
	wire transfer

CHAPTER 7

Special Events

"A special event is a unique moment in time celebrated with ceremony and ritual to achieve specific outcomes."

DR. JOE GOLDBLATT, CSEP

IN THIS CHAPTER YOU WILL LEARN HOW TO:

- Define *special event.*
- Demonstrate an understanding of the components of special events.
- Identify key event principles.
- Define the difference between on-site and off-site events.
- Understand the reasons why a DMC conducts a site visit.
- Identify the role of marketing and branding in event planning.
- Develop a basic plan for performance guidelines.

Most program development includes **special events.** These events are designed to enhance the experience of participants through the creative use of unique venues, entertainment, décor and its many elements, and the individual capabilities of host properties. Special events also represent the greatest opportunity for artistic and creative development by the DMC. The proportion of these events can range from simple themes indigenous to the area (e.g., Western, beach, or Mexican themes) to elaborate productions that include name entertainment, custom-built props, one-of-a-kind locations, and unlimited creative development. A DMC's reputation will often be defined by the scope and caliber of events it is capable of producing. These events also represent significant revenue opportunities, resulting in a competitive business environment, with services being offered by production companies, in-house décor departments, and local special event and décor companies.

Event Planning

Basic principles apply when planning events. These come into effect when a group first considers hosting an event. The key components in the preliminary stages of event planning include the analysis of the objectives and the determination of goals. Is the objective to launch a new product, celebrate a wedding, confer an award? Is the goal to make money, lure new customers, or just have a good time? Is the event related to a meeting or conference, or is it purely personal? Is it public or private? Does it revolve around a national sports team, or does it create team spirit among co-workers?

Events offer an opportunity to express ideas and objectives with a certain measurable outcome. There are as many good event formulas as there are personalities that plan them. Destination management companies carefully assess the client objectives, vision, abilities, interests, and budgets, and they plan accordingly.

The program planning includes event development, beginning with history of the event. What has the group done in the past? What was successful? What was not successful? Timelines are established and an **event profile** is completed, compiling necessary data including location of event, number of guests, date, time, food and beverage needs, entertainment, décor, planned program, participatory activities, audio/visual needs, production, and budget.

On-Site Versus Off-Site

On-site events are produced within the hotel, most presented as themed events that take place in the ballrooms, outdoor areas, or special event areas on property. Large resort properties are aware of the business potential inherent in these events and are aggressive in promoting their space and capabilities. The hotels have a vested interest in keeping business on site, due to the increased food and beverage revenue generated. Many of the larger properties have developed décor and entertainment departments specifically to capture this business. The majority of program itineraries will include events both on site and off, with the first and last evenings most often produced in the hotel, and alternative evenings presented in other settings.

Off-site events showcase facilities outside the hotel—including, but not limited to, local attractions, historical venues, museums, unique locations, estate properties, restaurants, galleries, parks, and other available areas. Although there is additional cost in most cases for transportation, the venues themselves can offer a great value due to the appeal of the location and the comparative impact of the experience. Locations are evaluated on a variety of factors, including proximity, travel time, capacity, capabilities, costs, weather risks, facility restrictions, and more.

There are multiple considerations in planning either type of event.

ON-SITE EVENTS

When planning an on-site event, first assess the availability of space for set-up prior to designing the décor elements. This can have a dramatic impact on what can or cannot be done with the time available prior to the event. Evaluate the consequences and backup location (if necessary) in case of inclement weather. Determine what can and cannot be accomplished and what is the time frame for last call in making venue selection. Be sure that the client is aware of these parameters prior to the event date.

Determine the hotel charges for rigging, power, and any other miscellaneous charges. Assess the status of labor unions in the hotel and its cost and effect on your set-up. Determine whether these expenses are your responsibility or will be billed to the client's master account. All of this must be approved in advance.

Determine noise limitations and curfews. Find out what other events are taking place near yours, and determine if they will encroach on your event (or vice versa) based on music, sound overflow, and so on. Anticipate solutions before problems arise.

Coordinate the style of food/beverage service with the theme/event design to be sure that they complement each other, as well as the goals of your client. Discuss and agree to a seating capacity and style, as it will have a significant impact on the event layout. Then develop a room layout/scheme so that all vendors and the hotel will be working from the same plan.

Evaluate the load-in capabilities and constraints (including dock access, elevator access, and openings). Also be aware of **strike** requirements—the time it will take to dismantle the event. Produce a comprehensive and detailed timeline, including pre-setting of entertainment equipment and a sound/light check.

Most important, have an on-site manager who is prepared to deal with challenges, changes, the client, and hotel personnel oversee all elements of set-up.

OFF-SITE EVENTS

Select an appropriate venue based on your client's goals, budget guidelines, capacities, capabilities, and transfer time. Then develop an appropriate theme, along with food and beverage service, entertainment, décor, and activities to enhance the venue.

Assess all permit requirements (if applicable) and special guidelines that affect the use of the facility. Will streets need to be closed? Must special parking arrangements be made? Does the venue have strict hours of operation that might affect your event? Is smoking permitted? Submit applications for facility permits at the earliest possible time and determine permit/usage fees.

Assemble a team of vendors whose combined expertise and professionalism assure the successful development and fulfillment of the plans. In order to maximize the profit of the off-site event, the DMC must be prepared to include all of the vendors involved in the event within the proposal. A great deal of research may be required to assure that the venue and vendors are a good match and will create a cohesive and successful experience for the client on the day/night of the event. Many hotels are now soliciting the catering for these off-property events, either directly or through the DMC. Consider the hotel's services when soliciting bids for food and beverages. Verify all vendor licenses and insurance coverage to adequately protect participants, hosts, and your company.

Develop and discuss a *weather backup plan* if the event is scheduled outside and will be at risk if there is inclement weather. Identify *last call* for implementing the alternative plan. Develop a comprehensive schedule of services that includes event layout, timeline, vendor list, and all critical aspects of the event. Advise the hotel of the arrangements and timeline so that it can coordinate the impact of the event within the hotel (including traffic at departure area and within restaurants).

Once again, have an on-site manager who is prepared to deal with challenges, changes, vendors, facility managers, and clients. The on-site manager will oversee all elements of set-up.

Selection of Appropriate Sites

For the DMC to make appropriate suggestions of off-site venues, it must get information from the client. What is the proposed date and time of the event? Is the date/time definite, or could accommodations be made? What is the estimated number of people (range of minimum to maximum)? What is the age range and gender ratio of guests?

What is the budget for the event? Many clients are unwilling to give hard numbers, but a DMC must have some idea of available funds in order to present an event that is appropriate to the client needs. Proposing an extravaganza including fireworks, custom props, and name entertainment to a client on a tight budget is a waste of time for both the client and DMC. The opposite is also true, in that balloons alone will not satisfy a client who is expecting a blowout gala. See Figure 7-1 for venue suggestions to fit any budget.

The DMC must also determine what type of transportation, if any, is desired. What are appropriate themes for the event? And, most important, what goals need to be accomplished? For example, if networking for attendees is a major goal, loud music throughout the event will be inappropriate.

The DMC must also research the particular rules and regulations of each site suggested. Some basic questions to the site include the availability of proposed dates. If they are available, put dates on hold. How long will the venue hold the date without a deposit, and is the deposit refundable? How are rental costs determined (e.g., by amount of guests, hours spent at the event, or amount of space used)? Are there restrictions on noise? Are certain items not allowed, due to security issues (e.g., cell phones, pagers, or cameras)? Is there a list of preferred caterers?

What is a common or unique venue will, of course, depend on your location. A movie studio will not have the same "unique" impact in Los Angeles as it will in Denver. Likewise, a beach makes more of an impression in St. Louis than in Miami.

Common Options

Art museums/art galleries	Local attractions
Historical museums	Zoos
Botanical parks	Restaurants
Clubs	Hotels
Wineries	Parks
Convention center	Beach or waterfront
Ships, boats, yachts (on the coasts)	Theme parks

Unique Options

Ships, boats, yachts (in the Midwest)	Sports stadiums or athletic fields
Private homes or estates	Farms
Movie studios	Airplane hangers
Racetracks	Specialty stores (Tiffany)
Closed streets	Warehouses
Factories	Haunted houses
Ranches	Roof tops

Figure 7-1
Event Venue Options

Are there other events on the same day that precede or follow your event? If so, is there any affect on load in or out? Will there be enough event-site staff available to you? Are there food or décor restrictions (e.g., red wine allowed? candles, balloons, trees, etc.)? Address HVAC (heating, ventilation, air conditioning) concerns. Make sure there is air conditioning for a summer event. How long will it take for room temperature to change once air-conditioning or heat is turned on? Is there sufficient electrical power for additional lighting?

Inquire about vehicle regulations. Are there specific drop-off and loading areas? Can streets leading to the venue accommodate buses? Will you have to pay to have meters covered with no parking signs? Will police details be necessary for traffic control? What is the venue's cancellation policy?

All of these concerns must be addressed before selecting a site. However, the financial rewards to the DMC of using an off-site venue make the time and expense involved in researching a variety of sites worth the effort. Every event is an opportunity to capture a percentage of sales that is not possible when the event is held on site.

Nevertheless, a word of caution is necessary. It is important to remember that the convention services staff at a hotel can be very helpful to you in securing a client's program. It is not in your long-term best interests to entice a client to take all evening events off-site. The hotel counts on this revenue as well, and in the end, it is beneficial to continue a relationship with a hotel long after the client has left your city.

The Site Inspection

The **site inspection,** the physical visit by the client and DMC representative to assess a property or facility prior to an event, is a major component of a DMC's "value-added" service. During this critical interaction with the client, the DMC has an opportunity to educate the client in regard to the positive aspects of the potential sites and, through past experience at the sites, alert the client as to any possible negatives that will affect the successful production of the event. The site inspection also affords the client an opportunity to assess the DMC's knowledge of local venues and understanding of event production pertinent to the client's specifications.

The client site inspection may take place at various points throughout the planning process. It could happen when the client is considering a number of destinations in which to hold a meeting, or it might take place when a client has chosen the destination but has not made a final commitment to a certain property. It can also take place after all hotel contracts have been signed when the final program itinerary needs to be completed. In any of these situations, the DMC can play a major role in helping to market and sell the destination to the client and/or final decision makers.

A comprehensive site inspection might be limited to event venues alone or might be expanded to include tour excursions being considered during the program. The site inspection can be as simple as inspecting one restaurant or as complicated as a motorcoach loaded with an association planning committee. See Figure 7-2 for a sample site inspection checklist.

Site inspections that last for more than a few hours and involve food and beverage service can add costs for a DMC. Before

After you have determined your possible event venues, you will need to compare facilities to judge the most appropriate site for the program. You must begin at the front door and work your way through the venue. The areas to concentrate on include the following:

Entrance	Lobby/front desk	Bell staff/valet
Corridors	Usable square footage	Loading docks/elevators
Lighting	Security	Parking
Restroom facilities	Emergency risk management	Permits and licenses
Insurance	Power requirements	Kitchen facilities
Special services	Staff	Entrances and exits
Cleanliness		

Figure 7-2
Sample Site Inspection Checklist

accepting the responsibility for the site inspection, the DMC needs to consider how many marketing dollars it is willing to invest in the procedure. A site inspection can cost several hundred dollars in out-of-pocket expenses, or it can cost several thousand dollars, depending on the scope of the services the DMC will be providing to support the program. An evaluation of the quality of the business must be made to determine whether the dollars spent will be worth the business. Often, incentive companies or third-party planners will make more than one site inspection for a program. An honest discussion with the client is a necessity so that ground rules can be set in advance as to how much of the site inspection expenses the DMC is willing to absorb, versus how much the client is willing to reimburse the DMC.

IN PREPARATION FOR THE SITE INSPECTION

Most clients will give you a very small window of dates for their site inspection. If you are not available, you have lessened your chance of capturing the business, and may not be asked to provide a proposal.

When preparing for the inspection, notify your client of the sites that will be visited and the time of arrival at each venue. Often, additional people will be contributing to the site inspection at different times of the day, and the client appreciates this pre-planned itinerary.

Determine the number of people who will accompany you on the site inspection and arrange for a driver and sedan or limousine to take you to the different sites. It is too difficult to focus on selling yourself and your company's capabilities as well as the virtues of the suggested sites while driving.

Make luncheon arrangements in advance, and make it clear to the client that you are the host. If your site inspection is to begin as soon as the client transfers from the airport, offer to meet the client at the airport rather than at the hotel.

Reconfirm with each venue as to the proposed date of the event as well as the date and time of the site visit. At this time, notify the **function manager,** the primary contact who represents the site, that no costs should be discussed in front of the client. If the client poses any financial questions to the function manager, the manager should defer to the DMC.

DURING THE SITE INSPECTION

If you are relatively familiar with the venue, try to conduct the inspection without the function manager accompanying the group. You will have more credibility at the site, as well as more control over the conversation.

If the function manager is included in the inspection, mention the general specifications of the event immediately after you introduce your client. The specifications include which space in the venue you want to use; the type of event, such as a reception, lunch, or dinner; the amount of people; and the date and time of the event.

At the conclusion of the inspection, be sure to determine exactly what specifications should be included in the proposal, and solidify the deadline proposal submission. As a follow-up, you should immediately send a thank-you note to the client, and honor the due date of your proposal.

VALUE-ADDED ASPECTS OF THE SITE INSPECTION

Provide the client with a disposable camera and offer to have the film developed. You can send the photographs with your proposal. Or use your digital camera to take pictures during the site inspection and insert the pictures into your proposal, as well as sending them by e-mail so the client will have them immediately.

Signing a Contract with the Off-Site Venue

Once the off-site venue is selected, it is imperative to secure it with a deposit immediately. The DMC should not put a deposit down on the venue without first receiving a signed contract and deposit from the client. The DMC, not the DMC's client, has the relationship with the venue. The contract should reflect this.

By definition, a contract is a promise or set of promises for the breach of which the law gives a remedy. All venues are unique and all events are unique; thus, contracts must be inclusive of all common elements and guidelines. The following elements should be included in a venue contract:

- Names of parties involved
- Dates of the event
- Type of event
- Description of event
- Charge for facility
- Deposit
- Payment schedule
- Exclusive contractors, if any
- Cancellation clause
- Liability clause
- *Force majeure* (an unpredictable event or occurrence out of the control of the contracting parties, and which is not attributable to any act or failure to take preventive action by the party concerned)
- Insurance requirements
- Rules and regulations
- Arbitration clause
- Acceptance of terms
- Competent parties (both parties must have legal capacity)

Marketing

Events extend the traditional boundaries of contemporary marketing and promotion. Until fairly recently, marketing focused primarily on exchanges of goods and services. Today, organizations, both for profit and not-for-profit, recognize universal needs for marketing their message. During an event, guests might be exposed to an entire marketing campaign through signage, entertainment, lighting, giveaways (gifts or amenities), and any countless manners of branding. As marketing was a generic activity, its application has broadened far beyond traditional boundaries. One category of nontraditional event marketing is **person marketing,** efforts designed to cultivate the attention, interest, and preference of a target market toward a person or group of people rather than a product.

Event marketing refers to the marketing of sporting, cultural, and charitable activities to selected target markets. It also includes the sponsorship of such events by firms seeking to increase public awareness and bolster their images by linking themselves and their products to the events.

The event to end all events, the Olympics, features 10,000 athletes from 198 countries who take part in 28 sports. The games can generate more than 1.3 million visitors to a venue. More than 1 billion viewers might watch a globally televised event. A major sponsor might spend $706 million for media rights and earn more than $800 million from the sale of advertising.

Marketing strategy has become a new element in the event planning process.

Music Licensing

When booking entertainment, it is important to understand the issues relating to the use of copyrighted music and to be knowledgeable about the associated responsibilities.

Copyright laws were passed to provide protection to creators of music, drama, graphic arts, and other literary and artistic creations. Under the law, *users* of music, whether live or recorded, are required to pay copyright fees. Under the definition of the law, *users* are defined as the sponsor of the event where the music is being played. Thus, a corporation that hires entertainment through a DMC or entertainment company for a function at a hotel is considered the sponsor of the event and is therefore responsible for **music licensing.**

When the use of music increased dramatically because of electronic broadcasting, a **blanket license** was created to meet the need. This need resulted in the formation of organizations to enforce the rights and collect fees for the use of music. The two major music-licensing firms in the United States are the **American Society of Composers, Authors, and Publishers (ASCAP)** and **Broadcast Music International (BMI).** These two organizations represent artists who hold the copyright to approximately 95 percent of the music written in the United States. Copies of the licensing agreement and reporting forms can be obtained from ASCAP at (800) 652-7227 or BMI at (800) 925-8451.

It is prudent to obtain licenses from both ASCAP and BMI because the list of songs covered under either organization changes continually, and it is difficult to obtain current and accurate lists. Obtaining licenses from both agencies also covers situations where music selections are requested from the audience.

In the early 1990s, ASCAP and BMI became aggressive about enforcing their rights to collect fees from the meetings industry, recognizing the potential for revenue from meetings, expositions, and conventions. For most events, the costs associated with music licensing are minimal. Both ASCAP and BMI assess fees based on the attendance at the event where the music is being played. Fees are not paid until the music is actually played.

Both ASCAP and BMI use spotters who frequently visit venues and investigate organizations that are unlawfully using licensed works. The penalties for using **unlicensed music** are substantial. Sponsors of events are ultimately responsible for music licensing; however, all producers of events should be knowledgeable about the requirements and what the responsibilities are.

Checklist for Event Planning

Special events are the bailiwick of many destination management companies. They give the opportunity to flex the creative muscle and are often the most memorable part of a program. DMCs can make or break their reputation based on the caliber of the special events they produce. Therefore, understanding the fundamentals outlined in this chapter is a must.

Figure 7-3 is a checklist to help you determine if you have covered all the elements required for a special event. Once you grasp the basics that are the building blocks of all special events, you are free to build everything from a cozy dinner for two to a sky's-the-limit extravaganza.

☐ A contract with the client has been signed by both parties.
☐ Venue has been selected.
☐ Cutoff dates are established.
☐ Appropriate reservation systems have been developed.
☐ Transportation needs have been determined and coordination is complete.
☐ Liability has been discussed and appropriate safeguards are in place.
☐ Rental arrangements have been made and delivery of items scheduled.
☐ Staging and production needs have been addressed. Coordination complete.
☐ Music licensing compliance has been arranged with ASCAP and BMI.
☐ Entertainment has been contracted.
☐ ADA compliance has been discussed with client. Appropriate arrangements have been made.
☐ Setup and space usage have been determined. Floor plan has been generated.
☐ Signage needs have been determined. Signs have been ordered or produced.
☐ All outside services have been contracted.
☐ Food and beverage arrangements have been made.
☐ Arrangements for audio/visual equipment and technicians have been made.
☐ Insurance and liquor liability issues have been addressed.
☐ On-site emergency preparations have been made and an emergency plan has been distributed to appropriate individuals.
☐ Seating arrangements have been addressed.
☐ Staffing arrangements have been made.
☐ The event theme has been determined and decor and prop arrangements have been made.
☐ Arrangements for communication with staff and client have been made. Additional equipment rentals complete, if necessary.
☐ Amenities have been determined and arrangements have been made.
☐ All suppliers have written instructions.
☐ A schedule of services has been generated and is ready for distribution.
☐ Pre-event evaluation with client complete.
☐ Post-event evaluation scheduled with client.

Figure 7-3
Event Planning Basics Checklist

Key Ideas

Special events offer the greatest opportunity for artistic and creative development of an event by a DMC. A DMC's reputation will often be defined by the scope and caliber of the events it is capable of producing. These events also offer significant revenue opportunities, resulting in a competitive business environment.

On-site events are produced within the hotel, and most of them are presented as themed events that take place in the ballrooms, outdoors, or special event areas on property.

Off-site events showcase facilities outside the hotel including, but not limited to, local attractions, historical venues, museums, unique locations, estate properties, restaurants, galleries, parks, and other available areas.

Site inspections are an opportunity for the DMC to educate the client in regard to the positive aspects of potential event sites, and for the client to assess the DMC's knowledge of local venues and understanding of event production pertinent to the client's specifications. Site inspection charges should always be discussed with the client in advance.

Special events offer a unique marketing and promotion opportunity. During an event, guests might be exposed to an entire marketing campaign through signage, entertainment, lighting, and giveaways. Person marketing is just one of the nontraditional marketing categories coming to the forefront.

Music licensing is an important component of events where music will be played. Sponsors of events are ultimately responsible for music licensing; however, all producers of events should be knowledgeable about the requirements and what the responsibilities are.

Key Questions

1. What are the differences between on-site and off-site events?
2. What is the vendor's role in a site inspection?
3. Who is responsible for site inspection charges?
4. Event planning basics may include a number of items. Referring to Figure 7-3, which items could apply to planning

an off-site event for 15 board members and their spouses? How would they apply?
5. Who should be knowledgeable about music licensing requirements and what the responsibilities are? Who is ultimately responsible for music licensing?

Key Terms

ASCAP
blanket license
BMI
event marketing
event profile
function manager
music licensing

off-site events
on-site events
person marketing
site inspection
special events
strike
unlicensed music

CHAPTER 8

Food and Beverage

"Food and beverage celebrates personal experiences. It is so vital to successful business networking and networking camaraderie. To my knowledge, there is no such thing as 'a virtual beer,' and until technology can develop that, you will never be able to replace the face-to-face interaction of meal functions."

JAMES R. POLHEMUS, CMP

ASSOCIATE DIRECTOR OF SALES

RONALD REAGAN BUILDING/INTERNATIONAL TRADE CENTER

WASHINGTON, D.C.

IN THIS CHAPTER YOU WILL LEARN HOW TO:

- Understand the disciplines of food and beverage planning.
- Realize the responsibility of destination management companies in food and beverage activities.
- Recognize the difference between various meal services.
- Understand diversity and culture in group meal planning.
- Realize the importance of understanding state and local alcohol laws.

Planning a lunch for 15,000? An executive board dinner for 10? Food functions are part of practically all programs and events. The basic elements of social food and beverage planning are consistent, no matter what size group. Attention must be given to determining the goals and objectives of each food and beverage (often referred to as **F & B**) function.

Food functions are scheduled during programs for numerous reasons. F & B functions satisfy basic nutritional needs during full days of scheduled activities. They offer opportunities for networking and relaxation and they are enveloped into themed events, ceremonies, commemorations, and social events as part of the celebrations. A multitude of food functions are commonplace in the industry, and can range from breakfast and breaks to brunch and lunch, from high tea to late-night suppers, from gala receptions to "grazing" events. **Grazing** refers to light, small snacking. Snacks can range from dry snacks such as pretzels or popcorn to more elaborate small dishes that are usually eaten with the fingers instead of utensils.

Destination management companies must be well-trained in food planning, as they not only act as consultants offering solutions to objectives, but also are responsible for the production of the function, the selection of the caterer, the room set-up, design elements, and rentals. Since logistics vary from meal to meal, venue to venue, and budget to budget, DMCs must understand every element of menu and F & B planning.

The efficient and cost-effective provision of food and beverage in all its various aspects represents the keystone of competitive and creative destination management. A huge topic encompassing much of every attendee's day, the subject requires a serious understanding of many disciplines, from wine and food connoisseur, to catering manager, to room designer and setup crewperson, to, occasionally, group psychologist.

Menu Planning

A word needs to be said about menu choices for your guests. Guests are becoming more adventurous in the foods they will eat, but a destination management company that wants to stay in business will do well to remember that the average person will eat only about 40 foods over and over again for his/her entire life. If you and your client agree to be creative, try to keep it to small bites at a reception or one course at a dinner. Too much creativity can make for very hungry people!

The choice of menus will depend on budgets, preferences, nutrition, size of group, length of event, and facility capabilities. Preset menus might not provide the selections that you need. Most caterers or chefs will offer additional suggestions or substitutions, or even custom-design the menu.

RELIGIOUS AND DIETARY LAWS

In considering food choices, a good DMC will remind the client to question more recondite food choices. As our audiences become more global and more sophisticated, there are more guests who will require special attention. Consideration must always be given to special needs, particularly religious or dietary special needs.

Muslim groups do not eat pork or drink alcohol, while Hindus do not eat meat from the cow family, poultry, fish, or eggs. You do not offer Muslims food between sunrise and sundown during the 40 days of Ramadan fasting. Jewish attendees may request **kosher** meals and may not eat pork, shellfish, or mixed meat and dairy. Mormons do not use alcohol, caffeine, or tobacco. Some Catholics may choose not to eat meat on Fridays during Lent.

There are two basic types of vegetarians. **Lacto-ovo vegetarians** do not eat meat, poultry, fish, or shellfish, but will eat eggs, cheese, and milk. **Vegans** do not eat meat, poultry, fish, shellfish, dairy products, eggs, or honey.

Health considerations must also be taken into account. More than 25 percent of adults are **lactose intolerant** (they cannot eat milk products). Many expect you to plan accordingly. Food allergies are on the rise, many of them life threatening. Nuts or wheat gluten might be taboo to certain guests. Always inquire about any restrictions or accommodations needed, and plan accordingly.

GEOGRAPHIC SPECIALTIES

It is recommended that you take advantage of the program location's specialties, such as Southern cooking in Atlanta, barbecued ribs and steak in Kansas City, or clambakes on the eastern coast. Localities may have laws that are particular to their region. Liquor laws vary from region to region or county to county. Some local health departments require certain laws for food handlers. Local convention and visitors bureaus or tourist bureaus can recommend local applicable offices for reference and verification of laws.

ADDITIONAL TIPS ON MENU PLANNING

When planning menus, consider the season. Seasonal fruits and vegetables are always fresher and more appealing. Lighter meals should be served in the warmer regions and summer months, while heartier and heavier dishes may be served in winter months. It is better not to serve foods that are likely to spoil in direct sun and heat. Food temperatures should be regulated and checked for safety levels before serving.

Demographics must also be considered. Men, on an average, eat more than women and prefer beef, while most women prefer something lighter such as chicken or fish. Statistics show that fresh vegetables are preferable to canned or frozen, while broccoli is still the number one choice of vegetable for both men and women. Tossed salads and Caesar salads are popular with both men and women. Regarding desserts, men prefer cheesecake and chocolate mousse, while women prefer fruit or cheesecake.

Balance your menu selections so that certain foods are not repeated. **Food stuttering** is repeating dishes meal after meal. Do not serve a chicken Caesar salad for lunch and then offer baked chicken for dinner. Try not to repeat meal offerings, such as a deli lunch three days in a row. Offer varieties when continuous meals are served.

Menu ganging, the process of utilizing the same types of foods that other groups at the same venue are using, can be a good negotiating tool when budgetary restraints restrict creative menu planning.

Even though a healthier and more nutritious lifestyle is the current trend, when traveling and attending meetings, seminars, and events, many guests will break all rules. They still tend to eat foods they do not normally eat and drink more heavily than they would at home.

Meal Functions

BREAKFASTS

Although breakfast provides a start for the day, many guests skip this meal. It is important to understand your group so that food and money are not wasted.

Continental breakfast is the fastest and easiest for the attendees. The breakfast consists of coffee, tea, and orange juice, plus muffins, Danish, croissants, or other types of breads or pastries. Guests serve themselves. This type of breakfast usually lasts for approximately one to one and a half hours. Many guests will arrive in the last 10 to 15 minutes.

A **full breakfast buffet** will contain two to three styles of eggs, two to three types of meats, a potato dish, four to six types of breads, muffins or pastries, a selection of hot and cold cereals, fresh fruits and juices, milk (whole and non-fat), and coffee and tea. This may be a good choice for a group of hearty eaters.

English breakfast expands on the full breakfast. All of the items from the full breakfast are available, as well as action stations for Belgian waffles, omelets, or crepes made to order for the guest.

Full-served breakfast requires more time than a buffet breakfast. The guests are seated and wait staff serve the meal. This type of breakfast might be served to kick off a meeting, for example.

REFRESHMENT BREAKS

Most meetings and conventions will offer their attendees a mid-morning and mid-afternoon break. This allows the guests to make telephone calls, use the restroom, and have something to eat and drink. A minimum of 30 minutes should be allowed for each break.

Breaks may be set up outside of the meeting room in the pre-function area if the space will accommodate the group. Breaks may also be set up inside the meeting space at the back of the room. Keep in mind the noise factor created by the staff during set-up and breakdown. There should be one attendant for every hundred guests, and the set-up should be completed at least 15 minutes prior to the break time to ensure that everything will be ready if the meeting breaks a bit early.

Menu choices will depend on the budget as well as the demographics of the group. Coffee, soft drinks, and bottled water are most often served at each break. Mid-morning breaks might also include juices, muffins, bagels, pastries, or yogurt. Afternoon breaks might include cookies, brownies, popcorn, soft pretzels, or fresh fruit. Keep in mind that healthy choices should be offered at each break. See Figure 8-1 for percentages to calculate for refreshment breaks.

Themed breaks are also an option. If the meeting has a theme or central motif, this may be carried out in the food served or the table decorations. The hotel may enjoy the challenge of a themed break and help you with ideas and suggestions.

Energy breaks are becoming more popular as healthy and fit lifestyles are more important to people. Healthy choices should be

Beverage	Consumption Percentage
Morning Break	
Regular coffee	55%
Decaf coffee	25%
Tea	10%
Soft drinks	25%
Afternoon Break	
Regular coffee	35%
Decaf coffee	20%
Tea	10%
Soft drinks	70%

Figure 8-1
Refreshment Breaks

offered at the breaks, which can include bottled waters, juices, sports drinks, granola bars, power bars, yogurt, or fresh fruit. A brief exercise break is sometimes included in the break time as well.

LUNCHEONS

Luncheons are provided for the convenience of the attendees. By providing lunch, you can keep the attendees from wandering too far from the meeting area and better maintain your time schedule.

Luncheons can be either buffet or served. A separate room should be provided whenever possible. If necessary, the meal can be served in the meeting room, but the noise of setting up and breaking down will be very distracting.

Boxed lunches or other working luncheons have become increasingly popular due to time and budget constraints. Be sure that the room is large enough to accommodate the appropriate set-up if you will continue a meeting during lunch. For example, you may need to set the room in a crescent shape rather than round tables so that attendees are able to view a speaker or slide presentation while they are eating.

Be sure to allow enough time if the attendees will be going off-site or will be on their own for lunch. Make sure that there are restaurants close by or that transportation will be provided.

Menus for any type of lunch should be lighter in fare, especially if a cocktail reception and dinner are planned for later in the evening. A larger meal may cause some attendees to feel sluggish in the afternoon and thus be less productive.

RECEPTIONS

Receptions are great opportunities for attendees to gather together to meet friends and co-workers, have general conversation, and network. Most receptions will be followed by a dinner. If a theme is planned, it is best to continue the theme throughout the evening.

Food for receptions may vary, based on preferences of the group and the budget. Foods that are high in protein and starch are better for receptions that will be serving alcoholic beverages as these foods allow for slower absorption of alcohol into the bloodstream. Foods that are salty, sweet, or greasy will encourage attendees to consume more beverages.

Seating at a reception should be limited, as you do not want guests to simply sit, eat, and drink. This is a time for networking and socializing, so seating should be limited to about 20 percent to 25 percent of the attendees.

Buffet tables may be set with various hors d'oeuvres and replenished as needed. Consumption of food can be lessened if the hors d'oeuvres are passed on trays. The hors d'oeuvres can be either hot or cold, depending on the budget. Either way, the food should be bite-sized and easily handled so that attendees can sample a variety of food items.

If you are on a limited budget, you might consider serving dry snacks as well as vegetable crudités, cheese cubes, or various chips and dips, salsas, and so on. Discuss the menu with the caterer for creative yet inexpensive menu suggestions.

DINNERS

Dinners can range from very informal to gala events, limited only by your budget and creativity. The dining area can be enhanced by adding lighting, sound, linens, centerpieces, and so on to carry out a central theme. Dinners may be served to the guests seated at a table or they may be served buffet style. Make sure that you have enough staff for either service type.

When choosing a menu, keep in mind the season, local cuisine, and specialties of the caterer. If a caterer is known for a particular main dish, you might want to highlight that and do something less extravagant with the dessert. Or you might want to focus on a local cuisine, such as Cajun. Of course, fruits and vegetables in season are always preferred.

Food Service Styles

Food service offers diverse opportunities at each meal or break. Distinct styles are defined as follows:

American service refers to plated meals prepared in the kitchen and served as a complete meal to each guest. This type of service still retains first place in the food service hierarchy.

Many meetings are adapting a more relaxed form of service for meals called **station service.** Small buffets are placed in various areas around the room, each offering different, complementary parts of the menu. The rationale is that this set-up encourages movement and promotes networking. A typical example would be for the menu to offer ethnic foods and to have a fajita station, a sausage and peppers station and a knockwurst and sauerkraut station located in different areas of the room.

Family service consists of large bowls and platters prepared in the kitchen and placed at tables set in the traditional fashion, allowing guests to help themselves (see Figure 8-2). This is an expensive form of service, since foods must be heavily laden on service plates so that the last person to avail him- or herself of the foods is not denied a portion. These types of meals are generally best offered when the foods are simple. A perfect example would be to offer a family-style farm meal at a State Fair Themed Event.

English service is similar to family service in that the vegetables and side dishes are placed on the tables (see Figure 8-3). The difference is the presentation of the main course, which is brought to the table on a tray or cart and presented to the host who either cuts the food or chooses to have it done by the server away from the table. The traditional American Thanksgiving dinner with the turkey presented tableside is an excellent example of English service.

Figure 8-2
Family Service
Courtesy of St. Louis Community College at Forest Park

Figure 8-3
English Service
Courtesy of St. Louis Community College at Forest Park

Figure 8-4
French Service
Courtesy of St. Louis Community College at Forest Park

French service, the most expensive in terms of service personnel, is generally reserved for very formal dinners. In this form of service, platters containing a variety of items are assembled in the kitchen; guests are presented with an empty plate and wait staff present the platters (see Figure 8-4). The waiter then serves the chosen items to the guest. Plated entrées and beverages are served from the right. Bread and butter, salad, and so on are served from the left. Everything is removed from the right. This style is very elegant, but it requires additional room for a waiter to serve and extra staff from the standard one waiter for two tables.

In **Russian service,** the food is prepared and cut in the kitchen and guests serve themselves from a platter presented by the waiter (see Figure 8-5). Each menu item is presented separately, and the waiter offers the platter from the left to each guest at the table, moving counterclockwise around the table, ladies first.

Figure 8-5
Russian Service
Courtesy of St. Louis Community College at Forest Park

Buffet service is when foods are arranged on tables and guests serve themselves and place foods on their own plates. Wait staff may be stationed behind tables to replenish food service plates and bowls or they may serve beverages.

Cafeteria service is very similar to buffet service except food is served from behind arranged tables by a wait staff rather than guests serving themselves (see Figure 8-6).

Butler service is a method of serving in which wait staff moves amongst the guests and serves food and drinks (see Figure 8-7). This is most commonly used for serving hors d'oeuvres.

Cart service refers to service in which foods are prepared at tableside, and servers design individual plates for each guest. Sometimes this service is used as a dessert cart.

Preset service is the arrangement of food, usually a salad, cold entrée, or dessert, on banquet or round tables prior to the seating of guests.

Figure 8-6
Cafeteria Service
Courtesy of St. Louis Community College at Forest Park

Figure 8-7
Butler Service
Courtesy of St. Louis Community College at Forest Park

Box lunch is a light meal served in a box that also contains condiments and utensils. Destination management companies use this type of food service frequently with tours and recreational programs, such as golf outings.

Meal Service

One of the DMC's most important pursuits is to make sure not only that the food and beverage is appropriately planned, but that the service is impeccable. The most highly regarded caterers are those that assemble their staff prior to a food function and completely prepare them for the event.

The wait staff should look clean and presentable and know the proper serving procedures. Clean uniforms, clean nails, the covering of body piercing and tattoos should be the normal requirement. They should never engage guests in conversation or interrupt table conversation. The wait staff should be fully informed of the meal inclusions, as guests often ask for a dish explanation. The wait staff should remember that some guests are critically allergic to some ingredients and be specifically aware of ingredients such as peanuts, wheat gluten, monosodium glutamate (MSG), or milk.

When using buffet service, have ample space for guests to maneuver easily. Use ample-sized plates and place all self-serving utensils in a methodical design. Make the service tables as attractive as possible utilizing floral centerpieces, custom linens, or accent lighting.

In ordering meals or suggesting them, try to remember that the cardinal rule in the catering business is "keep hot food hot, cold food cold." It seems so simple, but if your client books a long-winded speaker between the salad service and the entrée, you might find that it is not so simple. In a case like that, serve a large piece of food like a chicken breast, not sliced chicken, since thick pieces will retain heat better than thin ones. Whole vegetables hold the heat better than julienne cuts.

Food service protocol has changed over the past several decades. With the pursuit of healthier eating, the suggestions in Figure 8-8 should be followed to allow guests to make healthy choices.

- Serve sauces and salad dressings on the side.
- Label alcoholic ingredients if they are in dishes.
- Offer the option of margarine instead of butter.
- Use assortments of grain breads.
- Include fruit and yogurts.
- Use pastas.
- Avoid too many fried foods.
- Offer a variety of desserts, including fresh fruit.
- Offer regular and decaffeinated coffees.

Figure 8-8
Suggestions for Healthy Food Service

The preparation and servicing of any event includes far more than waiters and bartenders. Menu selection will have a significant impact on the portion of costs that are attributable to the personnel. Beef Wellington costs more than filet mignon, not only because of the cost of the fois gras, but also because a chef has to handle the meat twice and assemble the crust as well. When you order a meal, you will not want less than one waiter for 25 at breakfast and simple lunches, and one for 20 at multicourse lunches and all dinners.

Beverage Service

Beverage service—alcohol and nonalcoholic drinks—is an important part of menu planning at any food function. A thorough knowledge of beverage formulas, laws and restrictions, and types of service are necessary elements in every function.

NONALCOHOLIC BEVERAGES

Nonalcoholic beverages can include coffee and tea (both caffeinated and caffeine-free), bottled waters (carbonated or noncarbonated), soft drinks (with and without caffeine), power drinks, juices, milk products, and nonalcoholic beers and sparkling wines.

When serving coffee or tea with meals, it should be served separate from the meal, away from the table. Waiters should not lean over the guest to pour hot coffee or tea. After dinner, guests should have a choice of regular or decaffeinated coffee (served in designated coffee pots) with accompaniments such as pitchers of cream or other dairy enhancements, pure and artificial sweeteners, and coffee flavor enhancements (e.g., French vanilla, hazelnut).

In today's coffee-conscious society, plain-Jane coffee is not always enough to satisfy guests. Consider serving specialty coffees such as espresso, latte, and cappuccino. Espresso is a very strong coffee brewed by forcing pressurized steam through powdered dark roasted coffee beans. Cappuccino gets its name from the cap of foam on the top. It is made from one third espresso, one third steamed milk, and one third foamed milk. Café au lait and caffe latte are basically the same drink with either an Italian or French twist—a shot of espresso in hot steamed milk.

Amy Powell, CMP, meeting project manager at MAC Meetings and Events in St. Louis, Missouri, says that it has been her experience that beverage consumption has shifted dramatically in the past three to five years as the result of the changing demographics of attendees. More and more soft drinks and power drinks (PowerAde, Gatorade) are required and consumed at breakfast and morning breaks. Specialty coffees and a variety of teas (herbal, meditative, chai) are expected. Knowing the demographics of the group will make for a more successful F & B design and plan.

ALCOHOLIC BEVERAGES

The client and the program budget determine service of alcoholic beverages at functions. A good formula to use for budget calculations is that 20 percent of the overall food and beverage budget should be designated for beverages.

When planning any function with alcohol service, every organization should be aware of all applicable local, state, and federal laws and regulations regarding the possession, use, sale, consumption, and service of alcoholic beverages. It is the responsibility of a destination management company to have a strong working knowledge of the intricacies and liabilities of liquor control boards so that they can appropriately advise their clients. Some states give clients the right to bring in their own liquor to non–hotel sites and others do not. Some sites forbid the distribution of alcoholic beverages for money; it must be paid for prior to services at a site that is not the distributing bar.

Drinking patterns have changed drastically in the past ten years. Guests are drinking less and less, especially of hard liquors, while vodka remains the three to one favorite. Many health-conscious guests are ordering red wine and are becoming much more interested in what type of wine is being served. Expect to have guests ask for their wine by variety. The days of red and white are over. No longer is it acceptable to have just a regular and a light beer on the bar. Guests want variety and are clearly fascinated by microbrews and foreign beers.

SERVING WINE AND BEER

Serving wine at formal dinners differs from wine service at informal functions. See Figure 8-9 for wine service rules for both functions.

Beer etiquette should be given the same attention as wine service. Pilsner glasses, steins, or even oversized wineglasses are

---

The traditional wine service at a formal dinner should follow these rules:

- Sherry is poured into very small stemmed glasses to accompany a soup.
- White wine is served in the smaller of the two wineglasses.
- Red wine is served in the largest of the wineglasses.
- Red wine is served during a salad or cheese course.
- Champagne is served in a fluted goblet at the beginning of the dessert course.

When serving wine at informal dinners the following rules apply:

- Red wine should be placed on tables opened and allowed to "breathe" for at least 30 minutes prior to serving.
- White wine should be made available throughout the meal and served chilled or kept in an iced bucket.
- White wine should be served with appetizers, and both red and white should be offered with dinner.
- A chilled sparkling rose or sparkling white wine can be offered throughout the meal.

Figure 8-9
Wine Service

appropriate for serving beer. Never put cans of beer on dinner tables. Offer domestic, international, and nonalcoholic beer when using beer service.

AFTER-DINNER DRINKS

When serving after-dinner drinks, sweet liqueurs and brandy are served last, after the coffee has been served. After-dinner drinks should be served in the following manner: sweet sherry, port, or Madeira may be served in a white wineglass and are served at room temperature; sweet liqueurs such as Cointreau, Benedictine, or Sambuca are served in small-stemmed glasses at room temperature; Cognac and brandies are served in snifters.

CONTROLLING COSTS OF ALCOHOL SERVICE

Understanding the various types of bar service options will help control budgets, and satisfy program objectives.

A **cash bar (no-host bar)** is a private bar set-up where guests pay for drinks with money or drink tickets that have been purchased and have a drink value. The drink ticket or coupons may or may not include the gratuity on the beverage, depending on the client's preference. This type of bar will typically ensure the lowest amount of alcohol consumption. Bartenders and venue staff to collect tickets are paid separately. Cash bars can offer any variety of liquors, premium or standard (house) brands, beers (domestic and international), wines, nonalcoholic beverages, soft drinks, juices, and waters. The type of liquor offered is usually based on the history of the group's functions and the demographics of the group.

An **open bar (hosted bar)** is a private bar at which drinks are paid for by a sponsor or the host organization. Guests tend to drink more with open bars and costs are much higher. Formulas for calculating consumption for both cash and open bars can be found in Figure 8-10.

Charges to the sponsor or organization are billed back based on either per drink, per person, per bottle, and limited-consumption bar. **Per drink** (also called **on consumption**) is the process of charging for liquor served by the number of drinks served. Costs of drinks are predetermined and agreed upon by the organization.

Cash Bar

- 1.5 drinks per person if the cash bar is open for one hour during the average cocktail hour and light food is served
- 2 to 2.5 drinks per person is average for a cash bar during a one and a half hour reception with light food served

Open (Hosted) Bar

- 2 to 2.5 drinks per person for a one-hour hosted cocktail reception held after a meeting, at the typical cocktail hour, with light food service
- 3 to 3.5 drinks per person for a one and a half hour hosted reception with light food service

---

Figure 8-10
Calculating Liquor Consumption

By the person is when the organization pays a predetermined and agreed upon absolute rate for beverage consumption during the event. The per-person rate usually includes all beverages, including alcoholic beverages and soft drinks. This is typically the most expensive method of bar service. The advantage is that all costs are known up front, and this can help pre-establish an exact budget.

Serving alcohol **by the bottle** refers to liquor service charged for by the full bottle. Organizations pay for all bottles that have been opened, even though at the end of the event bottles are partially full. This plan is not as frugal as once thought, since unused liquor is charged back. However, if the organization is holding multiple events or hosting hospitality suites, arrangements can be made to utilize the remaining partially opened bottles.

A **limited-consumption bar** is when the organization mandates the maximum amount of money that it will pay for beverage service. This is based on a per-drink basis and the bar keeps a tally for a limited amount of time. When the tally reaches the agreed upon total, the bar is converted into a cash bar where guests pay on their own or with tickets.

There are many differences of opinion on bartender ratios within the hospitality industry. The Association of Destination Management Executives recommends one bartender for every 75 guests for ultimate service. If the group arrives in mass, one bartender for every 50 guests is preferred. For larger groups (over 500) you can reduce the amount of bar service staff to one per 100 guests and strategically place bars around the area so as not to create a bottleneck of guest traffic and to prevent long lines.

If bars are opened and closed from the rear of the event site, you will have far better control of traffic and consumption. In the early minutes of the event, the bartenders at the front of the room are stationed in front of their closed bars and direct guests to the rear of the venue, thus avoiding the bottlenecks that often occur at the first two bars. The subsequent opening of bars every 15 minutes from back to front will ease this problem greatly. At the close of the function, close the bars from back to front, starting some 20 or 30 minutes before the end of the event, marrying the leftover bottle segments into the front bars.

In some hotels, you may find hindrances to this procedure. Discuss it up front with your catering manager and suggest a call to the local liquor control board if you are told that combining bottles is illegal. Sometimes what is legal and what is not becomes part of the myth of the industry, and a suggestion that the information be checked with the authorities will bring a clearer perception between what is factual and fictional. In some cases, it will be possible through a negotiating challenge to have the partials left at the conclusion of an event assigned to first use at a later event, or sent to the hospitality room, if there is one. Note, however, that this requires very detailed record keeping. The responsibility is on you as the buyer to prove what liquor was left. Have the beverage or catering manager sign your inventory sheets in and out.

LIQUOR LIABILITY

According to the Professional Convention Management Association (PCMA), the organization providing alcohol to guests could be held liable if any of the guests become intoxicated and cause injury to themselves or others or damage to property, or if liquor is served to someone younger than the legal drinking age. See Figure 8-11 for precautions to take to keep guests from becoming intoxicated.

There are also **Dram Shop laws** in effect in most states in the United States that iterate the responsibility levels of all parties in-

Certain precautions can be taken to prevent guests from becoming intoxicated:

- Never allow guests to mix their own drinks.
- Do not allow the serving of doubles.
- Do not announce a "last call."
- Begin serving coffee at least 30 minutes before the end of the function.
- Have plenty of nonalcoholic options on hand so guests can more easily regulate their own consumption.
- Be sure to have food available throughout the function.

Figure 8-11
Tips to Avoid Guest Intoxication

volved in the distribution of alcoholic beverages. For your own safety and reprise from liability, make sure that the venue or caterer who will be dispensing alcoholic beverages offers training and certification to its bartenders and always carries an insurance policy that specifically covers the service of liquors, beers, and wines. If you are not part of the service of the alcoholic beverages (for example, the bar was ordered from or will be billed through your company), it is wise that you include specific language holding you harmless from any actions pursuant to such service in your contract. See your attorney about this very important and often-neglected clause.

While Dram Shop laws vary from state to state and even within states, there are at least four types of liquor sales that are illegal in the United States:

- *Sales to minors:* Liquor may not be served to anyone under 21 years of age.
- *Sales to intoxicated people:* Liquor cannot be served to anyone who appears to be intoxicated.
- *After-hour sales:* Most areas restrict the hours during which alcohol may be served or sold. Beyond those hours, serving or the sale of liquor is illegal.
- *Unlicensed sales:* A hotel's on-premises liquor license would not be valid for an off-premises event. A temporary license would be needed.

Food and Beverage Protocol

In the world of business protocol, the underlying objective for food and beverage functions is for the guest to come away from the event having had a fulfilling and memorable experience. There are etiquette procedures that should be followed as general rules, and all organizations and destination management companies should make these their official and prescribed techniques.

A **receiving line** is recommended when a majority of the guests do not know or have never met the host or the organization's upper management. A good rule of thumb is that it should not be used for attendance under 60 guests. The location of the receiving line must be crucially placed so as to not inhibit traffic flow or cause obstacles to entering the function. The time allotted to the receiving line staging depends on the length of the event. For two-hour cocktail receptions for large groups (500 or more), the receiving line should be available for one hour. The delegation of the line is critical. The line should be as short as possible, with the most important person/s positioned at the front of the line.

Assigned table seating and table cards are recommended for large groups. It enables organizations to strategically seat guests, helps identify no-shows so that waiters can remove place settings and distribute empty chairs so that there are no totally empty tables, and assists waiters when a variety of entrées are pre-selected, as the entrée selection can be coded on the place cards.

A **dais** is a raised platform for seating prominent people at the head table. Dais guests should be asked to meet prior to the dinner to familiarize them with the seating arrangement and to assign seats. Organizational hosts should be there to greet them, usher them to their seats, introduce them to any dais members that they may not know, and brief them on the dinner agenda. Each chair should be labeled. The guest of honor or the highest-ranking dais guest should sit to the right of the host. Never seat anyone behind the lectern.

GUEST SEATING

Calculating space needs for food functions is like piecing puzzle parts together. There are wonderful room diagramming software programs that will automatically calculate space, draw and configure tables and bars, show décor and plants, and make the process of room set-up much simpler.

According to Bill Campitell, Las Vegas Convention Planning Network, planners can avoid most of the logistical challenges of an F & B function if the proper formulas are applied well before the event. Blocking the correct space is only one of several areas that should be managed for a successful "sit-down" event.

When calculating with round tables in a room, you need to "square off" the measurements. Taking into account the amount of space needed for seated guests as well as space needed for aisles between the tables yields the linear feet needed for each table. See Figure 8-12 for linear footage standards.

Once you know the diameter of the table in the venue's inventory, you only need to get the dimensions of the clear seating area to determine the room's capacity.

Example: You have a room where the dimensions are 108 feet × 80 feet, and you are only using 6-foot (72-inch) rounds. There is no speaker or other activity in the room, and the meal is plated. As previously mentioned, 11 linear feet is needed for a 72-inch table.

Calculation:

$$108' \div 11' \text{ clear seating length} = 9 \text{ tables per row;}$$
$$80' \div 11' \text{ clear seating width} = 7 \text{ tables per row;}$$
$$9 \text{ (tables per row)} \times 7 \text{ (tables per row)}$$
$$= 63 \text{ (maximum number of tables)}$$

Now that you know how many tables fit into a room, determine how many people you want per table. For this example, 10 people will fit very comfortably around a 72-inch round.

60″ rounds	10 linear feet per table (seats 6 to 8 people)
66″ rounds	10.5 linear feet per table (seats 8 to 10 people)
72″ rounds	11 linear feet per table (seats 9 to 11 people)

Figure 8-12
Linear Footage for Banquet Rounds

Simply multiply the number of tables in the room by the number of people you wish to put at each table.

Calculation:

63 (total 72″ tables in room) × 10 (people per table)
$$= 630 \text{ (total people)}$$

Be aware that when using this formula, you might have to eliminate one table near each exit door to comply with local fire laws.

DANCING AND ENTERTAINMENT

When dancing and entertainment are to be included, a little extra work is necessary to determine the actual clear seating area after you have accounted for the dance floor and risers. Rarely is everyone on the dance floor at the same time. Using the formulas in Figure 8-13, you should be able to comfortably determine the square footage required for the dance floor.

Example: Your event is for 300 people with an average dance participation (50 percent on the dance floor at a given time).

Calculation:

300 (total guests) × 2.5 (square feet per guest)
$$= 750 \text{ (total square feet of dance floor needed)}$$

If the dance floor were close to square, its dimensions could be almost 27 feet × 27 feet × 30 feet. (*Note:* most floors come in 3 × 3-foot sections.)

To establish the table capacity of the room, subtract the number of tables lost to the dance floor space and bandstand from the total the room is capable of holding.

Percent expected on dance floor at one time:	Dance floor square footage needed per guest at banquet:
60%	3 square feet
50%	2.5 square feet
40%	2 square feet

Figure 8-13
Floor Space for Banquet with Dancing

When booking any entertainment to enhance the food and beverage function, consider the objectives and history of the organization. Live entertainers should be strategically placed so as to not interfere with the flow of guests. Soft live music or piped in quiet music is recommended during dinner. The purpose of dinner is for guests to interact and converse. **Sight acts** (performers who must be watched to be appreciated, such as mimes, jugglers, dancers, and acrobats) may be appropriate but also may be menacing to guests trying to eat.

Going the Extra Mile

Many times a client will have a preconceived idea of how a buffet should be set, what caterer to use, or which wine to select. However, the client's ideas might not always be the best choice. It will take careful consideration in approaching the situation and possibly additional details in planning.

For example, a client might want a buffet at a certain location in the room. It is then the planner's responsibility to explain why it would be better in a different location—traffic flow, accessibility, and so on. Or, if a client wants to use a particular caterer that you know will not be able to meet the needs of the client, you might suggest that they use the caterer for only a portion of the meal—allowing the planner to use other sources to create a better balance for the meal function. If a client wants to serve a particular wine, you might suggest a different wine to accent the entrée or a different entrée to complement the wine selected. Gordon Thompson, DMCP, partner at Cappa and Graham, Inc. in San Francisco, says, "We have learned that we often know more about wine and food pairing than many other caterers and restaurants. We also have great contacts in Napa Valley so we often assist our clients with food and wine, especially when it come to seasonal items."

Often, a client will have a theme in mind for just a portion of the meeting or event. If a theme has been planned, it is wise to incorporate that theme throughout the meeting, dinner, event, and so on. You can encourage the client by suggesting ways that would not only include the theme but perhaps encourage networking.

Liquor	Beverage Breaks	Hors d'oeuvres	Banquets
22–25 drinks/bottle	20 cups coffee/gallon, 1.5 cups/person	7–8 pieces/first hour	1 wait staff/ 20 guests
10–12 Martini-Manhattans/ bottle	1 quart juice = 5 glasses	6–7 pieces/second hour	1 wine sommelier/ 80 guests
5–6 glasses wine/bottle	16 glasses/gallon beverage	Steamship round of beef/ 100–150 persons	
5 servings mixers/bottle	1 wait staff/100 guests	1 pound dry snacks/ 6–8 people	
1 bartender/75 guests	It takes 15 minutes to draw 5 gallons of coffee from a single urn.	1 wait staff/75–100 guests	
1/50 for mass arrivals		Avoid salty foods and seafood	
1/100 for more than 500			
1 keg beer = 7 cases			

Figure 8-14
Fabulous F & B Facts and Formulas

For example, Sam Thompson, DMCP, president of metroConnections, Inc. in Minneapolis used a Chili Cook-Off as part of a State Fair theme. Attendees were able to sample the products that were showcased during the exhibition. And, added Thompson, "Attendees were able to question their suppliers face to face and have first-hand experience with potential product use."

Attention to detail is always of utmost concern. Having staff on site to supervise catering staff, check facility cleanliness, and so on will ensure a smooth program and protect the professional image you have worked hard to create. Liaison personnel from the facility, caterer, and others should also be on site for quick resolutions to any issues. According to Ellis Frater, DMCP, president of Dietrich: Destination Consultants, Inc., "In the case of off-site functions, we always have a staff member on site when the catering truck arrives to supervise the load in. We also require their salesperson be there to liaison with the catering staff. We have had to have staff dismissed because of attitude and replaced."

The success of the meeting or event and the satisfaction of the client will be the reward for going the "extra mile." Food and beverage functions are one of the more complex services offered by destination management companies. A thorough understanding of this information will allow you to make intelligent choices when suggesting F & B options to your client. The facts and formulas in Figure 8-14 may serve as a useful reference. Even if you are so busy that your dinner consists of a candy bar from the honor bar in your hotel room, you can be assured that the client and the client's guests will eat, drink, and be merry.

Key Ideas

Included in the various services that destination management companies provide is the thorough knowledge and ability to plan food and beverage functions. The range of knowledge includes understanding what types of food services are offered both nationally and internationally, and which service is appropriate to meet the client's activity objective. Some services, including French service, are more time consuming and require more staff. Meals may be offered in a more formal format or a simple buffet-style meal. Alcohol and beverage service also include various types of formats that should be considered as part of program planning, including:

- Hosted bar
- Serving drinks by the bottle, per person, or on consumption
- Cash bar

Since food and beverage play a vital role in program planning, careful consideration and execution of all meals is a major service of destination management companies.

Key Questions

1. What role does a destination management company play in group menu planning?
2. What type of food service would be best suited for a formal corporate board of directors meeting with 25 attendees, and why?
3. What is a Dram Shop law?
4. What is the most cost-effective way to order food and beverage for meeting breaks?

Key Terms

American service	English breakfast
box lunch	English service
buffet service	F & B
butler service	family service
by the bottle	food stuttering
by the person	French service
cafeteria service	full breakfast buffet
cart service	full-served breakfast
cash bar	grazing
continental breakfast	hosted bar
dais	kosher
Dram Shop laws	lacto-ovo vegetarians
energy breaks	lactose intolerant

limited-consumption bar
menu ganging
no-host bar
on consumption
open bar
per drink
preset service

receiving line
reception
Russian service
sight acts
station service
themed breaks
vegans

CHAPTER 9

Additional Services

"Destination management companies have always been an exceptional resource for highly skilled, dependable staffing support. Their employees have been members of our network database supporting meetings and events globally and their outstanding customer service training and results oriented approach to work ethics have enabled us to be successful in creating the 'right match' for our customers."

KATE ZIPF

MANAGER, CLIENT AND MEMBER RELATIONS

CURRENT TEMP°

IN THIS CHAPTER YOU WILL LEARN HOW TO:

- Recognize what additional services destination management companies can provide.
- Use additional services to achieve added value for your organization by providing creativity, stability, and integrity.
- Place your organization's image in the marketplace by showing all the facets of services it offers.
- Address the security issues that might arise with your events and programs, and to better address them from the start.
- Understand the common staff structure of destination management companies and the job responsibilities of various employee positions.

Understanding Objectives

An understanding of the client needs and objectives will drive the information and fulfillment of services necessary to successfully plan and execute any program. Program basics may vary from client to client, so a thorough assessment of interests, program history, and experiences is necessary to analyze product and services solutions that fit the budget and the overall development of the details.

Understanding Competencies

Knowing your organization also involves knowing what you are and are not capable of doing. Every destination management company has a set of aptitudes and natural skills that it performs well. Self-assessments, goal setting, performance results, and constructive feedback from clients and vendors help DMCs identify their capabilities. Common competencies of a DMC include tours, ground transportation, special and themed events, and airport meet and greet.

Additional services provided by destination management companies can include any or all of the items in Figure 9-1.

Entertainment	VIP services	Gifts and giveaways
Staffing	Registration	Staff support
Housing services	Meeting planning	Security
Child care programs	Sports activities and recreation	Meeting planning
Marketing collateral	Name badges	Office furniture and office equipment rentals
Contracted services		
▪ Florists	Telecommunications	Technology support
▪ Photographers	support	
▪ Exhibit support		

Figure 9-1
Additional DMC Services

VIP Services

According to the Webster Collegiate Dictionary, a VIP is defined as "a person of great influence or prestige; especially: a high official with special privileges." VIPs can include heads of state, dignitaries, corporate leaders, rock stars, board members from a trade or professional association, sports figures, brides, and so on. The client will designate who is a VIP for each particular program.

Within the destination management industry, **VIP service** is defined as a system of providing special assistance to a high-ranking official or important guest. VIPs are clients that you value and want to thank or impress. This can be in the form of (but not limited to) accommodations, transportation, or amenities. The care and tending of VIPs can be time consuming and detail oriented. You must be prepared to meet the challenge. You must understand the needs of business and recognize how the client's organizational image is projected through professionalism. You can create an impact or be so discreet as to go almost unnoticed.

All the terms above suggest that a VIP requires special handling. What special services are typical for VIPs? Different services are, of course, offered by different entities. VIP travelers can expect special waiting rooms and check-in lines, free upgrades, free drinks, and preboarding privileges from an airline. Hotels may offer special check-in, room upgrades, concierge services (keyed elevator, guest club, gym accessibility, dinner reservations), hotel limousines for transfers, welcome baskets, wine, and other gift items.

What special handling would a DMC offer clients? Limousine pick-up at airport to their hotel, a welcome room gift, private tour of the city, lunch or dinner gratis, recognition throughout the year (e.g., birthday and holiday gifts), and regular mailings (e.g., newsletters, personal notes, Web updates) are just a few of the items a DMC may offer its VIP clients.

Name entertainment almost always requires special handling. VIP services may include a chartered private aircraft to and from the venue city and limo pick-up (airport, hotel, and venue) for the entertainer and entourage. Premiere hotel rooms for their entourage, dinner arrangements for all, personal security, and special bag handling for instruments may also be expected. A dressing room for the star, specialty catered items for the dressing room, and a break room for the entourage are almost always necessary. Special requests are often made. For example, black roses are required in the dressing room for Elton John.

Ensuring the anonymity of high-profile program attendees, often a company's chief executive officer or a big-name keynote speaker, has quickly become a priority for many clients. A DMC needs to put together detailed plans to prevent problems in this regard well in advance of the program date. And don't forget the often overlooked reminders listed in Figure 9-2.

Some VIPs will be more demanding than others. In many cases, you will need to "go the extra mile" (or more) to satisfy their requests. Many times a VIP is not as important as he/she thinks, or

---

1. Register high-profile persons with pseudonyms.
2. Provide plans for having these individuals enter or leave a hotel without having to appear personally at the front desk.
3. Make sure all paperwork related to such individuals is guarded. Many hotels will shred such paperwork immediately on checkout, as an added precaution.
4. Talk to the security firm you may be hiring for your event to determine what extra procedures may be recommended for key individuals.
5. Include discussions relating to "high-profile guests" as part of initial negotiations with a hotel, if possible. The property may have suggestions as to how they have dealt with similar matters in the past.
6. Talk to other meeting and event professionals to see what they have done. Attention to these areas has increased dramatically in the past year, and hard, fast guidelines have yet to be developed.
7. Depending on who your guest is, consider whether an armed guard should be used. As in most security matters, an ounce of prevention is worth a pound of cure.

Figure 9-2
Seven Tips for Guarding Information on High-Profile Attendees
Business Travel Executive, Sept. 2002, based on an article by John J. Fleming, The Brosnan Group

perhaps individuals think they should be treated as a VIP when, in fact, they are not. In these cases, it might be best to spend a little extra time with the person rather than elevating the person to full VIP status. For example, rather than sending the VIP gift basket to the room, you might personally call and offer to make dinner reservations.

When a VIP doesn't receive what was promised, you need to rectify the situation immediately. For example, if the gift basket was not delivered, or a sedan instead of a limo appears to transfer the VIP, let the VIP know that you are aware of the situation and that you will resolve the issue.

When a VIP becomes extremely difficult (for example, screaming at you over the phone) it is necessary for you to remain calm. Try to meet with the VIP face to face and let the person know that you are genuinely concerned about the problem and are sincere about a resolution. Let the VIP know that you are taking corrective action to resolve not only the problem, but also to make sure that it won't happen again. Perhaps one of the best rules in dealing with VIPs is to never promise more than you can deliver, but always try to deliver more than you promise.

Entertainment

Understanding the basic needs and objectives of a program will indicate the entertainment requirements. Fulfilling entertainment requirements can be as simple as hiring local talent such as jazz combos, pianists, magicians or other sight acts (performers who must be watched to be appreciated), or as complex as hiring major feature entertainers or even bringing an entire Broadway show into the venue.

The purpose of entertainment at a program is to keep attendees and/or guests amused, enthralled, and captivated. Entertainment is a great enhancement to programs that should be discussed with clients so that the selected talent meets budgetary considerations, group preferences, and objectives. Selecting inappropriate entertainment can not only disrupt the program, but also generate discomfort among the group. Consideration should also be given to the volume of music. Very loud music can interfere with conversation. If using a comedienne or humorist, material should be prechecked to avoid content that could be distasteful or offensive to the client and attendees. If using any type of musical talent, request samples in DVD, video, or taped format, along with any promotional photos and marketing pieces.

When booking entertainment and making final arrangements, riders should be carefully reviewed before signing any legal agreements. A **rider** is a clause in addition to an artist's contract stipulating special requirements for travel, dressing rooms, or technical equipment.

When using any type of live or recorded music, **music licensing** must be considered. According to the American Society of Composers, Authors, and Publishers (ASCAP) and Broadcast Music Inc. (BMI), an official sponsor or organizer of an event, or the entity that bears the financial responsibility for the event, is responsible for obtaining a license for the use of protected music from either or both ASCAP or BMI or other rights-licensing organizations. According to these organizations, the only exceptions are personal events such as birthday parties, weddings, bar and bas mitzvahs, and events attended by personal friends and family.

Amenities and Gifts

Amenities and gifts can add perceptual enhancement and bring a sense of importance to a concept, theme, celebration, VIP arrival, or other event. Presentation is always key. When choosing, wrapping, and/or adorning an **amenity,** it is important to be clear about its intent and about the recipient. Decorate and present it to convey overt as well as subtler meaning(s). Timing of an amenity is paramount. Often, amenities are given as a welcome gift to your client or as arrival gifts to your client's guests. Amenities might include small gifts given to tour guests as part of an organized tour, or party favors or promotional items at the place setting at a meal function. Another good use of amenities is to create a centerpiece incorporating novelties or food items that are meant to be shared by the guests at the table and then taken with them when they leave.

Gifts are an important part of the DMC experience. They can be the presents you bestow upon your clients in appreciation for their patronage. They can also be the presents your client gives to certain important members of the group they are hosting at the convention.

Occasions for gift-giving may include blitz gifts for hotels, CVBs, continuing clients, and others who can refer business to you. You should always include secretaries, assistants, concierges, and other **gatekeepers** when you give blitz gifts. These people can often give you valuable information. Note that it is wise to call hotels, CVBs, and other entities and get approval before you blitz. Some have policies against receiving gifts or limits on the monetary value of the gifts.

A gift might accompany a proposal and showcase your amenities as another part of the services you offer. A welcome basket (perhaps waiting in the client's hotel room, or given when you meet the client at the airport) is a great way to make a good impression. Gifts are also appropriate as a treat to be enjoyed in the middle of a chaotic meeting (e.g., snacks, bottled waters, or sweets), all cleverly packaged as a "Meeting Planner's Survival Kit."

A *bon voyage* present is always welcome. An excellent example here is a basket that includes bath salts, herbal teas, aromatherapy products, and so on, packaged as a "Recovery Kit." Gifts are also appropriate as a form of "thank you" for a client's patronage or as a "peace offering" when things perhaps did not go as perfectly as they should have. This is an excellent segue to open up the lines of communication and ease the tension of the situation. It often has the effect of "solving" the problem in the client's eyes.

A gift should *always* be thoughtfully considered and should include elements that show you know your client's individual tastes. It should be something the recipient will use and enjoy. Care should be taken to avoid "advertising" with a gift, because this has the air of promotion. However, feel free to include nuances that suggest your services in a subtler manner.

Some occasions when your client may prevail upon you to provide gifts for programs include welcome gifts for the superiors/board members/clients, or rewards for team-building or incentive activities. Clients may also request promotional gifts (e.g., at a trade show) or gifts to their staff for a job well done.

The program contents may dictate that gifts be utilized as raffle prizes or be auctioned at a party (e.g, casino parties often end with an auction where guests can bid on prizes using their winnings). Gifts may also tie into a themed event or **turn-down service,** when beds are prepared for sleeping and bathroom linens are usually replaced.

Staffing

A knowledgeable and committed staff is fundamental to the success of all destination management companies. In the simplest terms, DMCs are service providers. Although they represent a multitude of opportunities and services, it is through their *customer service* that they reassert their value to clients and to the industry.

Companies vary greatly in size, depending on their market and market share. However, almost all companies implement a fundamental staff structure that supports their business. Variations occur to meet the specific business demands, but these basic requirements are constant. See Figure 9-3 for a sample organization chart that shows the typical DMC hierarchy.

To date, there has been almost no formal curriculum for entry into destination management. In the past five years, progress has

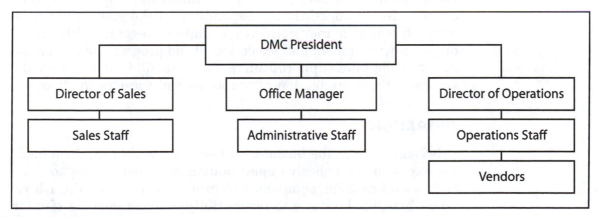

Figure 9-3
Sample Organization Chart

been made with the introduction of college courses that include destination management. Almost all training is through work experience.

Staffing requirements generally include all the following departments and/or job descriptions.

ADMINISTRATION

The **administrative staff** is responsible for the business administration of the company. This includes personnel/human resource management, technology/IT support, accounting, and general office management. In small companies, administration may interact with clients to some extent. In larger companies, they will work most closely with their own staff and will have limited contact with clients.

SALES

Sales departments vary in size and structure. **Sales managers** are responsible for developing and driving the business opportunities for the company. They are the most visible representatives of the company's services, meeting with hoteliers, convention and visitors bureaus, incentive houses, meeting planners, association planners, and other prospective business contacts to market their services. They work with their internal support teams to develop and present comprehensive proposals to their prospective clients. Sales managers are most often the ones to conduct site inspections when clients visit the destination. Depending on the size of the company, they may (or may not) have operational responsibility for the ongoing development and execution of the program. Most companies provide sales support team members to aid in the creative development and production of proposals and services to clients.

OPERATIONS

Sales can bring in the business—operations will bring them back! An experienced, cohesive **operations department** is the key to a DMC's success. For companies to grow and to maintain a loyal client base, the burden and responsibility of customer satisfaction is placed on the shoulders of the operations staff. Once the services have been defined by the sales team and brought to contract, the operations department steps in to move the program forward. Again, the method can vary from company to company, but in all cases, the operations expert is focused and dedicated to delivering the program at a high level of proficiency, on budget, and to the customer's satisfaction.

The goal is to transfer the confidence first established through the sales process to the operations process. Operations works closely with the client to finalize the many details of the program in the final days of preparation. Final menu selection, guarantees, itineraries, and other such details are reviewed and confirmed. The operations staff provides the on-site support and assistance to the client to guarantee the program delivery. It is their responsibility to keep sales informed of any and all developments that might require their involvement. At the program's conclusion, the operations staff will participate in the production of the final invoice and accounting to the client.

PROGRAM MANAGERS

In addition to internal personnel, most DMCs utilize the services of outside **program managers** to implement their programs. There are many different titles used (tour guide, program manager, destination specialist, or field manager, to name a few), but they all represent the person-to-person contact between the DMC and the participants. Often, these people work on a freelance, contract basis, working for multiple companies in a destination. Training for these positions is most often provided by each DMC, outlining the particular behaviors and procedures expected by that company. A few companies are able to hire staff on an exclusive basis, eliminating their availability to competitors. In the last few years, there has been an ongoing effort to establish a professional association for these tour staff in the hopes of raising the standards of professionalism and establishing best practices.

MEETING MANAGERS

More and more destination management companies are providing full-service meeting management. A **meeting manager** is a person whose job it is to arrange every aspect of planning and conducting a meeting or convention. When utilizing a DMC for meeting management, qualifications should be examined closely. Experience, certification (Certified Meeting Professional–CMP or Certified Meeting Manager–CMM), and a list of meeting-based clients should be part of the selection criteria.

Housing Services

Some destination management companies offer housing services. **Housing services** provide meeting planners with assistance on securing and managing appropriate accommodations with hotels, as well as monitoring and adjusting housing blocks throughout the process. DMCs that provide housing services have experienced reservations center staff who have experience in hotel bookings. Technology has completely redefined the housing process utilizing Internet-based technology to ease the process and offer immediate confirmations.

DMCs, along with their clients, set housing policies and procedures to optimize room blocks and use informative housing forms that ease the reservation process. Most housing services also provide toll-free call centers with local and international telephone numbers, fax, and on-line reservations. Staff then confirm attendee reservations, send rooming lists to hotels at the appropriate cutoff date, and assist with late registrants. Measurement reports are provided weekly, monthly, or whenever the client needs them. DMCs might also provide an on-site housing desk if required.

Contracted Services

Destination management companies are a great source for contracted services. Their utilization of local vendors and contractors gives them extensive knowledge and buying power for outsource supplier services. Several types of services might be included with contracted services:

- Florists
- Décor
- Photography

- Print collateral and badges
- Office furniture
- Office equipment
- Telecommunications
- Trade show support services

Security

Destination management professionals need to consider what sort of security protection and physical precautions may be appropriate for their clients. Security planning should begin in the earliest meetings between the planner and the destination management contact. Security should be modified and updated regularly to fit any diversions from the original plan.

The DMC may choose to hire a professional **security service company.** These companies provide security guards for such things as the entrance to a trade show or a special entertainment event where tickets or badges are required for admittance. These companies also provide around-the-clock security services for areas where exhibits and/or valuables are being displayed on consecutive days.

Off-duty police officers are often an option to direct or control public traffic entering an area where large-scale transportation movements are taking place. Off-duty police officers also provide a direct and vital link to the city's police department and other emergency services, such as ambulance and fire departments. Plain-clothed security officers are often required to monitor special concerns such as works of art, cutting-edge technologies, and even VIP attendees and celebrities.

Risk management/insurance companies offer vital services such as assessing facilities, emergency systems, and auxiliary items such as props, tents, lighting, electrical cords, and vendors (e.g., electronic bull, working race cars, and catering where open flames are required). These companies can assist you with specialized insurance (if needed), and with professional advice on how to limit or even remove the hazardous elements from your program.

Street festivals, 5K runs, and other special events will need attention to traffic flow, crowd control, and protection from criminal activity and other hazards. It is important to include the local police department in the early planning stages; indeed, their input may be a prerequisite for obtaining the necessary city permits.

The appearance of government officials, dignitaries and VIPs at your special events may necessitate inclusion of the Secret Service, FBI, or other governmental agencies in order to plan the security for the event. You might need to make the venue and vehicles available early so that bomb-sniffing dogs can search them.

Technology Support

New technology has resulted in new goods and services for DMCs, as well as all consumers. The Internet is transforming the way companies promote and distribute products. Destination management companies are monitoring new technology and successfully applying it to enhance customer services. They are able to support client programs through applied technologies such as databases, electronic data interchange, and interactive promotional techniques to more effectively create on-site solutions for registration, housing, badges, and so on.

Key Ideas

Additional services are elements one can use to market and support program enhancements to his/her organizational meetings and/or events. Destination management companies are able to offer the best value on additional services because of their logistical recognition, buying power, and local network contacts. A knowledgeable, well-trained, committed staff is fundamental to the success of all destination management companies. Since destination management education is just now emerging in academia, most DMCs have learned from experience and intra-industry cross training. Program managers or tour staff often work on a freelance, contract basis, and customer service is the point of distinction in which DMCs reassert their value to clients and to the industry.

Key Questions

1. What amenities would you offer as a welcome gift for attendees for a corporate meeting?
2. How would you market amenities to clients?
3. When would it not be appropriate to give or receive a gift?
4. What are the merits of having program managers?
5. What are the responsibilities of DMC sales managers?
6. What should be the primary focus of all staff members?

Key Terms

administrative staff
amenity
gatekeeper
housing services
meeting manager
music licensing
operations department
program manager

sales manager
security service company
rider
risk management/
    insurance companies
turn-down service
VIP service

CHAPTER 10

Pricing Strategies

"We work with professional destination management companies because they are reliable and they go the extra mile to get the job done. They have volume buying power and they pass those savings on to us, which saves us money on our budget."

JANET BOSSCH

INTERNATIONAL VISITOR PROGRAM MANAGER

MONSANTO COMPANY

IN THIS CHAPTER YOU WILL LEARN HOW TO:

- Identify several methods of budgeting/charging for services.
- Compute various methods effectively.
- Determine which are most commonly used methods and in what situation each applies.
- Distinguish between traditional and new strategic budgeting.

Developing an understanding of the pricing and budgeting process and becoming skilled at this function is fundamental to the success of every DMC. Clients are requiring different pricing procedures to coincide with their business practices. In the sales development process, it is critical that the method of pricing/budgeting be discussed so that information is provided in an acceptable format.

If all businesses had the same needs, the same basic environments, the same program objectives, and the same program profiles and attendees, budgeting would be an easy process. But in the real destination management world, program components are far too varied and complex to standardize into one simple budget. DMCs have three options:

1. They can simplify their approach to match one of the industry standard pricing systems and accept the consequences of deviations.

2. They can use in-house systems that can handle the basics based on historical programs and clients.
3. They can invest in third-party software that provides more flexible functionality.

Technology has redefined a sophisticated precise model for checks and balances and other controls.

Software programs can effectively accommodate unique variables and difficult calculations that give the client a budget that more closely resemble the client's business model. With cost-center pricing for clients, DMCs can also perform balance sheet planning and add service and goods costs at the click of a button.

Being able to implement a system that truly personalizes each individual program and provides clients a true financial planning analysis tool is necessary for a successful program.

Pricing Methods

There are several methods of budgeting/pricing services. Each method has its pros and cons, and some clients have a distinct preference for one form over another.

COST PLUS

This type of pricing shows the actual cost for services, plus a mutually agreed upon service fee (i.e., cost + 20 percent). Cost plus 20 percent service and coordination fee is used most often for items such as name entertainment (20 percent markup or less), photography, golf, **dine arounds** (use of a number of restaurants for one client with reservations and billing arranged by the DMC), and bar or other items on consumption.

Cost-plus pricing is revealing your costs and adding a fee separately, which can be calculated as a percentage, an hourly or daily rate, an arbitrary management fee, or a combination of these. See Figure 10-1 for cost-plus examples.

PACKAGED PRICING

Packaged pricing does just what its name implies. It packages multiple services, vendors, and costs together to provide a service. Direct costs plus gross percentage "profit" is factored into the price

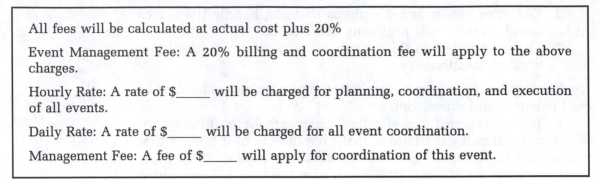

All fees will be calculated at actual cost plus 20%

Event Management Fee: A 20% billing and coordination fee will apply to the above charges.

Hourly Rate: A rate of $_____ will be charged for planning, coordination, and execution of all events.

Daily Rate: A rate of $_____ will be charged for all event coordination.

Management Fee: A fee of $_____ will apply for coordination of this event.

Figure 10-1
Cost-Plus Pricing Examples

to client, representing an all-inclusive charge (e.g., tours, price per person). The budget includes guidelines for minimum and maximum number of guests, all inclusions, duration of services, and any other factors that influence price. Packaged pricing is commonly used on tours, recreational activities, and off-property evening events.

MENU PRICING

Menu pricing is often used in more complex events that include multiple elements and a wide range of variables. Special events are often priced this way, with each major category identified, and the appropriate profit factored into each element. This allows for greater flexibility on the part of the client and simplifies the process of repricing. It also helps to identify those costs that do not change (e.g., venue rental, entertainment, lighting, and so on) and those that are affected by the number of participants (food and beverage, centerpieces, linens, etc.). Menu pricing is commonly used for on-property theme décor and entertainment.

FEE-BASED

This is the least-used method of budgeting, but it is applicable at times. A **fee-based pricing** of services will be agreed to prior to program development and based on time and expertise. This is also used at times for fundamental services such as *dine-arounds*. Many clients don't want to see the fees. This happens because the DMC is often a third-party vendor. The DMC's client may be a management company or incentive house that must report back to its own client, the company hosting the program. If the client must show the DMC invoice to the host company, a management fee will be undesirable. When using fee-based budgeting, DMCs must be wary of under-valuing their time and the service they are providing. The knowledge, experience, and contacts of a professional destination management company are extremely valuable.

The following figures highlight the various budgeting methods. Figure 10-2 is an example of cost-plus pricing. Figure 10-3 shows an example of packaged pricing. Figure 10-4 shows an example of menu pricing.

GRAND OPENING EVENT

Budget Summary

PROGRAM MANAGEMENT
Following is the cost for program administration management.

	Hours (Est.)	Standard Rate	Standard Cost
Strategic account manager	16	$135	$2,160
Marketing operations manager	8	$125	$1,000
Program manager	16	$115	$1,840
Financial analyst	3	$115	$345
Project manager	16	$100	$1,600
Program Management Subtotal:			***$6,945***

PURCHASED SERVICES
All prices include sales tax and gratuity where applicable.

Rental package	$15,500
Décor package	$14,795
Food, beverage, and catering tent	$31,025
Entertainment	$ 2,000
Purchased Services Total:	**$63,320**

EVENT MANAGEMENT
See attached proposal for details and line item pricing options.

Figure 10-2
Example of Cost-Plus Pricing
Courtesy of The Meeting Manager

Under the Sea . . . At the Stephen Birch Aquarium
(4 Hours)

Discover the spectacular **Stephen Birch Aquarium,** perched on the bluffs overlooking *La Jolla,* "the jewel" of the Pacific shoreline. This facility presents the underwater world of sea creatures in realistic habitats and allows visitors to experience the frontiers of marine science through interactive exhibits featuring both shore and ocean studies. It provides a fascinating insight into our mysterious, underwater world. The view is magnificent, spanning the Pacific coastline including La Jolla Cove and Scripps Pier. Upon arrival, guests may explore all of the exhibits, aquariums and the outdoor tidal pool. Themed background music will enhance the peaceful atmosphere.

A delicious food station dinner will be served at tables elegantly set with rich turquoise linens crowned with exotic floral centerpieces featuring a hand-blown glass fish. Washes of cool blues and greens will fill the walls, enhanced by water-like movement and kelp-shaped projections.

This Program includes:
- Exclusive, round-trip transportation via deluxe motor vehicle
- Scripps bus parking fees
- Exclusive use of the Stephen Birch Aquarium
- Docents to provide facility tours
- Full bar set-up and service (beverages billed on consumption)
- Complete food station dinner
- Coordinating food station decor and florals
- Themed tropical, aquatic centerpieces
- Washes of cool lighting in the dining area and functional lighting in the tide pool area
- Rental of tables, belly bars, chairs, linens, china, & glassware
- Stereo system & selected music
- Uniformed event directors to provide complete program coordination and on-site assistance
- All applicable taxes and gratuities

Price Per Person: $214.00
Based on a minimum of (100) guests
All beverages to be billed on consumption plus a 20% billing and coordination fee.

Figure 10-3
Example of Packaged Pricing
Courtesy of The Meeting Manager

California offers a lifestyle and cuisine all its own. Tonight travel **California's Highway 101** through the diverse regions of California and sample the charm and cuisine that has become synonymous with each of these areas. A large, black Astroturf highway with traffic signals and green highway signs of famous California destinations leads guests into the reception.

The highway continues past food-station vignettes depicting famous California destinations, inviting guests to sample the diverse flavors of California. Dinner tables will be dressed in green "road sign" color linens with black highway runners and topped with metal die-cast cars for centerpieces. Bars will be decorated to resemble roadside service stations, complete with road maps, oilcans, tires and custom service station signs. Tall, realistic palm trees created with burlap-wrapped trunks and topped with large, live palm fronds will be interspersed throughout the room continuing the coastal atmosphere. Colorful up-lighting will create an interesting palm shadow effect on the walls and ceiling.

Whether it's the laid-back lifestyle of the beach, the fruitful vineyards of Napa, Sonoma and Temecula Valleys, the wild times at the San Diego Zoo or Wild Animal Park, the stars of Hollywood, the Desert's simple elegance, San Francisco's Chinatown, or the exclusive shops of Beverly Hills, California offers something for everyone!

RECOMMENDED DECOR PACKAGE:

Entrance
Outside the event area, we will place our dramatic highway style entrance arch. Chrome trussing will form a 10' × 10' arch, which will be accented with green highway signage designating each of the California highlights represented in the food stations. Colorful up-lighting will complete the look.
   Price: $1,175.00

"Highway"
A black, Astroturf "highway" will guide guests into the event.
   Price: $295.00

Perimeter
Vignettes designed with a variety of highway theme decor such as signs, foliage, and faux rocks will enhance the overall theme.
   Price: $1,175.00

Perimeter (Palms)
Tall palm trees created with burlap-wrapped trunks and real palm fronds will be placed around the perimeter. Each will be washed with vibrant up-lighting, creating an interesting palm shadow effect along the perimeter walls.
   Price: $1,940.00

Figure 10-4
Examples of Menu Pricing
Courtesy of The Meeting Manager

Stage Decor

Our blue sky and beach backdrop will be enhanced with a lush foliage package consisting of fresh and faux palms and lush greenery.
   Price: $1,470.00 (Hotel to provide stage riser)

Tables (Based on 72″ rounds)

The hotel's 72″ tables will be covered in "highway-sign" green linens and topped with highway-style table runners. On each table is a 10″–12″ die-cast metal car on a plastic base.
   Price Per Table: $103.00

Cocktail Tables

Vibrant green linens will top each of the cocktail tables. Each will be centered with a whimsical streetlight. (Price includes table rental.)
   Price Per Table: $63.00

Belly Bar Cocktail Tables

Waist-high belly bar cocktail tables will be covered in black linens and tied hourglass style in the center with a yellow sash. Each table will be centered with a burst of colorful, coordinating florals. (Price includes table rental.)
   Price Per Table: $74.00

Chairs

Black wood folding chairs will be placed at each cocktail table and dining round.
   Price Per Chair: $4.25

Food Stations

Each of the food stations will be individually designed to represent an exciting aspect of the casual lifestyle typical of California. We will combine florals, fabrics and props to create a dynamic effect. Choose from the following options.
   Price Per Food Station: $440.00

Malibu Beach

A bright orange lifeguard chair will center this food station. It will be topped with a colorful umbrella and accented with bright florals in beach buckets, beach towels and other theme decor.

Old Town

A Mexican-style market cart brimming with fresh produce and buckets of cut flowers will provide the focal point for this station. Brightly-colored serapes and coordinating solid-colored fabrics will complete the look.

Hollywood

An old-fashioned mouse-eared camera, film reels, clapboard and red-rose arrangement will be featured at this food station.

Figure 10-4
(*Continued*)

Napa Valley
A large wine barrel, a winepress, and a dramatic basket arrangement will be accented with tapestry fabrics.

Mojave Desert
Desert plants and rocks will be combined with native style pottery and fabrics at this station.

Beverly Hills
This station will be designed with vibrant floral arrangements set inside a variety of shopping bags from famous Beverly Hills shops such as Giorgio and Armani. A large Rodeo Drive street sign will provide a central focal point.

San Diego Zoo
A bamboo arch will create the foundation for a dramatic display of tropical florals and foliage, accented with animal print fabrics and fuzzy white monkeys.

Sea World
A giant, whimsical, exotic fish "swimming" through fresh sea-like foliage will be incorporated with faux rocks, shells, and water-like fabric.

Point Loma
A 10′ tall lighthouse, complete with a rotating beacon light, will center this station. Lobster traps, fishing floats, and an assortment of shells will complete the look.

Bars
The hotel's rolling bars will be designed to represent vintage-style gas stations, complete with brick facades accented with shelves of gas station items such as quarts of oil, car parts, etc.
   Price Per Bar: $220.00

Lighting
Warm, sunset-color washes around the perimeter of the event will provide a vibrant glow.
   Price: $1,100.00

Special Notes: *Transportation, sales tax and labor are applicable to all decor elements.*

Transportation costs for this event will be billed on actual usage. Final transportation charge will reflect final event configuration.

California sales tax and labor charges will be billed based on final event configuration. Decor labor is charged at 22% of the decor, and lighting labor is charged at 30% of lighting decor. All labor and tax charges will reflect final event configuration.

Figure 10-4
(*Continued*)

Decor elements described above were available at press time and remain subject to availability.

Power, distribution, and rigging to be provided by hotel. These charges, if applicable, may be billed to the hotel master account.

ENTERTAINMENT OPTIONS:

Disc Jockey
Price: $700.00
Based on (3) hours

Caricaturist
Price Each: $225.00
Based on (1) hour

Walk-Around Magician
Price: $400.00
Based on (1) hour

OPTIONAL DECOR ENHANCEMENTS:

Perimeter Palm Enhancement
Additional, smaller palms (8′), fresh fern banks and faux rocks will turn each perimeter palm into a dramatic vignette.
Price: $880.00

Food Station Enhancement
Custom road signs will complete each food station.
Price Per Food Station: $74.00

Bar Enhancement
Custom signage will be on each bar.
Price Per Bar: $148.00

Vintage-style Gas Pump at Bar
Circa 1940—pump is in excellent condition.
Price: $515.00

Special Notes: Transportation, sales tax and labor are applicable to all optional decor enhancements.

Transportation costs for this event will be billed on actual usage. Final transportation charge will reflect final even configuration.

Figure 10-4
(*Continued*)

> *California sales tax and labor charges will be billed on final event configuration.*
>
> *Decor labor is charged at 22% of the decor, and labor is charged at 30% of lighting decor. All labor and tax charges will reflect final event configuration.*

Figure 10-4
(*Continued*)

Beyond Budgeting—New Budgeting Strategies

Much has been said about traditional financial management and how current management accounting fails to support beleaguered managers in today's competitive world. Simply adapting new methods such as fee-based costing may not bring the expected benefits that fit with the organization's infrastructure and style. When organizations try to use different pricing models to be more productive, the results fail to focus on the customer and the customer's requested pricing model.

In most organizations today, intellectual capital forms the greater part of the market value. **Intellectual capital** is the untapped, unmapped knowledge of organizations that has become the company's greatest competitive weapon. It is found in the talent of the people who work there; the loyalty of the customers it serves and learns from; the value of its brands, copyrights, patents and other intellectual property; the collective knowledge embodied in its cultures, systems, management techniques, and history. These vital assets are not found on a balance sheet, are rarely managed, and are almost never managed skillfully.

This shift in emphasis demands new forms of accounting and new ways of managing and measuring performance. Front-line managers are the entrepreneurs, strategists, and decision makers, constantly creating and responding to new opportunities for the business. Middle managers and operations support staff are more lateral integrators building competencies within the organization. And high-level management provides inspiration and the vision.

In this new accounting management, each department manages its own finances as if it were an independent company. This model makes all employees entrepreneurs, thus improving responsiveness through lateral integration. At the center of this new model lie processes and teams. Many firms have already adapted a process-based approach to management in an attempt to align their operations with the needs of the customer in mind.

An example of this new strategy is a contract-based DMC based in St. Louis, Missouri, MAC Meetings and Events. The company's success is built on its respect for its people and the belief that, at whatever level in the organization, its people will make the right decision. Department managers are encouraged to run their operations as if they were independent businesses. Once thoroughly trained, managers receive financial reports by contract. Because they are at the front line, treated as professionals, and rewarded on team profitability, they exercise a control over costs that is far tighter than a financial controller could ever exercise remotely. With this philosophy, MAC Meetings and Events has grown from a local DMC to a global business with multiple locations. It has grown its business 300 percent within one year.

The underlying philosophy in this new accounting process is one of maximizing value rather than minimizing costs, and the focus of measurement systems is on strategic performance, value-adding processes, and knowledge management and empowerment. Most of all, this model is based on trust between managers, support staff, customers and partners.

Whether they recognize this new management process or not, many organizations have already adopted many of the elements of this model, incorporating decentralization, empowerment, and economic value added.

In this new strategic pricing model, there are three traditional budgeting purposes:

1. *Forecasting and resource allocation:* In the new process model, front-line units will have direct access to capital, and are encouraged to share productive capacity across the organization. Managers prepare quarterly plans, and these are used for case forecasting but not cost control. The important distinction is that while traditional budgets are fore-

casts, they are also commitments. In the traditional systems, managers must participate in a bureaucratic and time-consuming process to build their knowledge of and commitment to the figures against which they will be controlled. In the new model, forecasts are prepared quickly, updated when required, and constrained by the annual planning cycle.

2. *Measurement and control:* Even though performance responsibility and accountability are delegated to the lowest level, it is still important that senior management monitor cash flows and have up-to-the-minute information on profit margins and performance. Assertive performance targets will be set, but month-to-month measures will not be based on "actual versus budget" reports, but rather, on strategic milestones and relative measures.

3. *Cost management:* In the new model, successful cost management is gained by creating a culture of frugality and continuous improvement, reinforced by an organizational reward system. Many DMCs are now educating their employees to understand such issues as which work is most profitable and which work adds value, and then helping employees identify and eliminate non-value-adding work. Again, the emphasis is on managing value up rather than managing costs down.

Even though many organizations today still function with traditional budgets, as we move from the Industrial to the Information Age, new budgeting offers a compelling alternative to organizational change and new strategic financial models.

Avoid Pricing Pitfalls

One of the biggest pitfalls that service providers make is letting emotions get in the way of economics. No company stays in business by offering services for free. It is too easy for clients to plead with DMCs to just add six more shrimp per person to the buffet, add more props to fill the room for an event, or ask the band to play for 30 more minutes for no additional fees. Destination management companies are reputable, professional companies with operating expenses, and they should be treated as such. DMCs should communicate their pricing and billing structure to the client to ensure that they are in agreement regarding procedures for additional charges. Negotiated rates with vendors, representing discounts on normal rates, should be carefully monitored for accuracy in the budget process.

Many DMCs have **contract addendums.** These are typically triple-mount (carbon) forms that list program additions after the contract has been signed. The addendums list what services have been added, whether before the program or on site, the date of the add-on, and the client's authorized signature for the order. Once completed, the client is given a copy and the originals are kept with the client file for final billing. Add-ons can be as simple as a role of packing tape or as complex as an entire event.

Successful pricing/budgeting is less about doing things right than it is about *not* doing things wrong.

Key Ideas

Developing an understanding of the budget process and becoming skilled at this function is fundamental to the success of every DMC. Clients are requiring different budgeting procedures to coincide with their business practices. In the sales development process, it is critical that the method of charging/budgeting be discussed, so that information is provided in an acceptable format.

Negotiated rates with vendors, representing discounts on normal rates, should be carefully monitored for accuracy in the budget process.

There are several methods of budgeting/charging for services—cost plus, packaged pricing, menu pricing, and fee-based pricing. DMCs must be competent in each type of pricing, and know when each type is applicable to an event.

Key Questions

1. Discuss why you would use different types of pricing for different types of functions.
2. What are the advantages of per-person pricing versus menu pricing?

3. Why are clients requiring different types of budgeting procedures?
4. Give an example of how menu pricing can simplify the budgeting process.
5. Site two benefits of "new strategic budgeting."

Key Terms

add-on costs	fee-based pricing
contract addendums	intellectual capital
cost-plus pricing	menu pricing
dine around	packaged pricing

CHAPTER 11

Technology

"Working with partners, including DMCs, it is imperative that they can digitally communicate with my staff and me anytime. That includes remote connectivity, e-mail and wireless capabilities. My designated DMC understands my company culture and works with our guidelines and ways of doing business effectively."

ROBERT SACKETT
MARCOM MANAGER
ENTERPRISE MARKETING
CISCO SYSTEMS

IN THIS CHAPTER YOU WILL LEARN HOW TO:

- Recognize how the Technology Revolution has affected business in general and DMCs in particular.
- Know the difference between hardware and software.
- Recognize what basic types of software most DMCs use to work more productively.
- Recognize what basic hardware is necessary for a DMC.
- Define several ways to effectively utilize technology within the DMC field.
- Recognize what basic security systems you need to protect your network.

The Technology Revolution

Dramatic changes in the last decade have affected the way business is conducted. New methods replace old rules; technology language has produced new words and old words have new meanings; the Internet has become the ultimate 24-hour communication device; e-commerce has turned virtual reality into reality, transforming business and customer relationships. Like it or not, this is the **Technology Revolution.** We have moved from the industrial society to the information society.

Startling statistics support the growth of computer and Internet usage. According to the U.S. Department of Commerce, Economics and Statistics Administration, U.S. Census Bureau, the computer has become a basic tool at work, school, and home. More than one in three U.S. households has a computer. In October 1997, 37.4 million U.S. households (36.6 percent) had computers. This is up substantially from 22.8 percent in 1993, 15.0 percent in 1989, and 8.2 percent in 1984.

Almost three quarters of children used a computer someplace. More adults use a computer at work than at home or school. Of the 92.2 million adult computer users, more than 63.9 million used a computer at work, compared with 56.4 million at-home users and 10.5 million adult school computer users.

Among all at-work computer users, word processing remains the most common use of computers on the job, at 57.0 percent. Other common work uses are keeping customer records and accounts (50.7 percent), e-mail and communications (47.0 percent), calendar/scheduling (37.5 percent), databases (34.1 percent), spreadsheets (32.4 percent), and bookkeeping (30.2 percent). Another major use of computers that has grown rapidly in the past decade is accessing the Internet. One in five Americans now uses the Internet. (Most estimates in these statistics came from data obtained in October 1997 from the *Current Population Survey* (CPS).) Additional statistics about the technology revolution can be found in Figure 11-1.

Technology has revolutionized the methods and speed of doing business. One of the greatest challenges to DMCs in the twenty-first century is to effectively use technology to improve services, improve response time, manage databases, provide operational business data, and manage extraordinary amounts of information particular to each client and program.

The Internet has made it much easier to access information in order to research client profiles. In addition, it provides an excellent forum for presenting company history and pertinent information to support business development and retention.

The marketing of company services and capabilities is changing from print media to electronic media, with Web pages providing a spontaneous, global window to our product.

The number of Internet users in China is estimated at 1,750,000.

1,700,000 copies of the Starr Report were downloaded from CNN in the first two days it was available.

Delta Airlines is planning to charge a $2.00 fee for tickets *not* purchased on the Internet. Amount of Delta Airlines tickets sold via the Internet in 1998: less than 3 percent.

Estimated U.S. consumer spending on online retail purchases during 1998 holiday season is $8,200,000,000.

There are 19 members of the U.S. National Advisory Commission on Electronic Commerce.

25 percent of retail stock trades now take place on the Internet.

Estimated number of Web users in the U.S. (May 1998): 57,037,000.

It took 5 Vanderbilt students to create the Muhammad Ali Web site.

There are no Internet service providers (ISPs) in Saudi Arabia.

Businesses in Britain and Ireland estimated the cost of dealing with spam e-mail at $8 billion.

In 1998, 3.4 trillion e-mail messages were delivered to 81 million e-mail users in the United States. That's more than 6.5 million messages per minute.

48 percent of employers think the Web has raised productivity.

Approximate number of page views at Yahoo: 38 million per day.

Estimated number of e-mail messages that were sent in the year 2000: 6.9 trillion.

Approximate number of new domain name registrations: 85,000 per month.

Figure 11-1
Technology Statistics (1998)
Source: www.why-not.com/company/stats.htm

      The faster business grows, the sooner DMCs must react to evaluate and address their technology needs. Realizing that technology and e-business affects every aspect of business, DMCs are transitioning traditional business models to cutting-edge e-business. E-business offers unlimited opportunities; by conducting a thorough needs assessment of systems, hardware, software, Internet, PCs (per-

---

Phone system with voice mail (including remote retrieval capabilities)

Fax machines

Pagers/cell phones

Desktop or laptop computer for each employee

E-mail (internal/global) for messaging and transmission of information, proposals, critical information

Internet access for research of clients, vendors, and services

State-of-the-art Web page for marketing/sales/service opportunities, with consistent updates

Basic software including word processing, spreadsheet, and database components

Digital camera for spontaneous transmission of venues, sites, etc.

Figure 11-2
Basic Technology Requirements

sonal computers), networking, and telecom, DMCs can take advantage of these opportunities.

For companies to remain competitive in this technology-driven market, fundamental tools are necessary to meet the expectations of clients. Compatible integration and utilization of hardware and software is critical to successful communication between parties. Many technology components can increase the productivity and credibility of your communications. Detailed next are some of the components and their considerations. See Figure 11-2 for a list of the most basic requirements.

Software

Webopedia.com defines **software** as computer instructions or data. Anything that can be stored electronically is software, but when people use the term software, they are most generally referring to the computer instructions. The distinction between software and hardware is sometimes confusing because they are integrally linked in that you cannot use hardware without software and you must have the hardware in order to store the software. A recent anonymous quote making the tech circuit is, "Those parts of the system that you can hit with a hammer are called hardware; those program instructions that you can only curse at are called software."

Software is often divided into two categories. **Systems software** includes the operating system and all the utilities that enable the computer to function. **Applications software** refers to the programs that do real work for users. For example, word processing, spreadsheets, and databases management systems fall under the category of applications software.

BASIC SOFTWARE REQUIREMENTS

Basic applications software requirements for any business will include, at a minimum, word processing, spreadsheet, and e-mail programs. **Word processing** represents 95 percent of desktop work and is used to generate text-based documents such as proposals, contracts, letters, tariffs, and the schedule of services. It can also be used to create business forms and templates and allows the DMC to insert graphics and photos for objects such as menus, name badges, venue pictures, and maps.

Spreadsheet software allows the user to create and electronically manipulate tables of data consisting of columns and rows of individual cells. Spreadsheets are the ideal choice for any application involving the manipulation of numbers since they allow you to input formulas that perform the required calculations automatically. Most DMCs use spreadsheets for invoices, expense reports, pricing, and budgeting. They are also an ideal choice for arrival/departure manifests since they offer the option of sorting items in chronological order.

E-mail, short for electronic mail, allows for swift communication and document transfer using communication networks. Although e-mail capabilities may be confined to the computer network within a single company, known as an **intranet,** most companies utilize an Internet connection to allow communication on a global scale. Messages are received on the other side of town or the other side of the globe in a matter of minutes or seconds. In addition, most e-mail programs also include features for task assignment, resource management, and a calendar with appointment scheduling. Adding the option for remote e-mail access will allow workers to stay connected while traveling or working from home.

The advent of e-mail as a basic mode of communication has opened many avenues for DMCs. In addition to the ease of communication between client and DMC, e-mail can be marketed as a tool for increasing program attendance. Elaine Wagner, CMP, CSEP, director of operations for MAC Meetings and Events in St. Louis, says, "As a matter of course, we now offer electronic invitations, or **e-vites,** as a service to our customers. A link to the invitation is sent via e-mail to prospective program attendees. These unique invitations feature music and motion and are much more attention-grabbing than your average paper invitation. All the standard information is provided, and they tie in wonderfully with online registration. The attendee can merely click on another link within the e-vite and register immediately. And they offer the added bonus of being able to track who has "clicked" their invite."

ADDITIONAL SOFTWARE

Although it is listed as an addition, **antivirus software** is fast becoming a basic necessity in business. This software searches the hard drive for viruses and removes any that are found. When using antivirus software, it is important to remember that new viruses come out almost daily and the software is only effective if it is updated often, preferably on a daily basis. Most antivirus software allows you to auto-update and download virus definitions in the background, rather than manually instructing the software to do so.

Database software organizes data in a logical manner so that desired data can be quickly retrieved. You might compare a database to an electronic file cabinet. Traditional databases contain fields, records, and files. A **field** is a single piece of data; a **record** is one complete set of fields; and a **file** is a collection of records. For example, your address book can be compared to a file. Each person's complete set of information is a record, and each individual piece of information such as phone number and ZIP code is a field.

Within a destination management company, databases are used to automate record keeping. They keep details about clients, contacts, suppliers, venues, and staff. Databases can also be used to track activity using dates and numbers. It might seem that databases merely replicate spreadsheets, but databases are much more powerful and somewhat more complex than spreadsheets. Databases were built to accommodate advanced reporting and data analysis that spreadsheets just cannot handle.

For example, if a DMC uses a database to store attendee information about a client program, in addition to sorting flights by arrival time that could be done in a spreadsheet, the DMC can also query the database to determine which attendees are attending a particular tour or breakout session. Are they all from the Midwest? Are they all female? This kind of information can help the client to make choices about program content.

Room-diagramming software allows a DMC to design the physical space for an event, including room/area dimensions, furniture size and placement, and so on. Standardized icons are used to represent tables, chairs, audio/visual gear, and even trees. Some room diagramming software offers options that will let you design an event down to the tabletops, showing placement of each wine glass, fish fork, and napkin. In addition, most programs will let you import CAD (computer-aided drafting) schematics from hotels and other venues to use as templates. This means that you can start with a diagram of an empty ballroom obtained from the hotel and add all your décor elements.

Another useful program to have is **photo-editing software.** With this software you can create photo galleries of events, venues and supplier offerings. You can modify, crop, and re-size photos to include in proposals. When combined with desktop publishing software, you can generate unique mementos of events for clients. **Desktop publishing** is more sophisticated and costly than word-processing software, but it allows you to embed illustrations and graphics directly into the text and gives you more control over margins, typefaces, and graphics. The software contains preformatted templates and designs that allow you to create Web sites, banners, signs, newsletters, brochures, business forms, gift certificates, business cards, and many other collateral items.

Online registration software allows you to customize program Web sites and manage attendees in a centralized database. The information is quickly accessible, and detailed reports can be created. The software allows you to send individual and batch e-mails, manage housing efficiently, and coordinate multiple tasks on behalf of your client and attendees. Most online registration software includes cash-management and payment-processing capabilities. Utilizing online registration can "wow" your clients with the added benefit of using your company.

Now that you are utilizing all this wonderful software, creating file upon wonderful file to make your clients happy and your life easier, what happens if the roof leaks and trashes your lovely new computer? You go right back to work—if you have used backup software. When combined with the proper hardware, **backup software** copies data and compresses it so that it requires less space to store on tape or disk. The amount of data you are backing up will determine how you store it. Data can be stored on compact disk or, for larger companies, magnetic tape. It can then be restored in case of hardware failure, accidental deletion, or disaster such as flood or fire. Backup is most effective if it is done frequently, preferably daily. And the backup tape does you no good if it is lost in the same fire that destroys your computer, so keep the backups in a different location than your computer. When it comes to backup, the cardinal rule is "back it up and move it out."

When purchasing any software, there are several points to consider. Make sure that any software you purchase is compatible with your operating system and that you have the minimum system requirements to effectively run the program. Be wary of $19.99 bargain software. If it is so outdated that it won't run on your system, it's not a bargain.

You might also consider if off-the-shelf software is the best choice or if a custom-designed program will better suit your needs. For tasks such as word processing and e-mail, off-the-shelf is usually the best bet, since compatibility with your client's programs is of the utmost importance in this case. However, processes such as online registration and Web site development (discussed later) may warrant investing in custom options. Like any other supplier, request references from software programmers and check them out. Ask questions and give details about exactly what you need the software to do for you. Don't be intimidated by technical jargon. A good programmer should be able to explain in plain language exactly what will be accomplished by any software to be designed.

Hardware

According to searchHP.com, **hardware** can be defined as "the physical aspect of computers, telecommunications, and other information technology devices." The term arose as a way to distinguish the "box" and the electronic circuitry and components of a computer from the program you put in it to make it function. Hardware includes not only the computer proper but also the cables, connectors, power supply units, and peripheral devices such as the keyboard, mouse, audio speakers, and printers.

PERSONAL COMPUTERS

Personal computers are also known as microcomputers, desktop computers, and laptop computers. TechWeb defines a **personal computer** as "a computer that services one user in the office or home." The acronym PC is often used, but with one distinction. The term **PC** generally refers to an *IBM-compatible* personal computer to the exclusion of other types of personal computers, such as Macintosh. Woe be to the person who refers to the techie's Mac as a PC!

When selecting and purchasing personal computers, take into consideration the basic job functions of each employee. In general, adhering to the principle of "the fastest goes to the neediest" will serve you well. This usually means that the secretary who creates documents, prepares spreadsheets, and utilizes desktop publishing software will need a faster, more powerful system than the president of the company, who e-mails and generates memos, but generally delegates technical work. Consider laptops rather than desktops for salespeople and program managers who travel often.

SERVERS

A **server** is simply a computer on a network that manages network resources. Servers are generally faster and more powerful than personal computers so that they can manage resources for multiple users. Servers may store files or manage printers or network traffic. Large networks may require separate servers for each of these functions, while one box may be sufficient for smaller DMCs. In what is referred to as a **client/server environment,** the file server holds most data for all users (clients) to share. In this type of environment, the server is the ideal location for a backup drive, allowing all files to be automatically backed up from one location.

PRINTERS

Invest in a good black-and-white "workhorse" printer that you will use for most documents. If you share printers over a network, multiple users can use one faster, more expensive laser printer instead of purchasing multiple desktop printers. Since color can add value to proposals through the inclusion of photos and graphics, invest in at least one good color printer or printer copier. Combination printer/fax/scanners can be inexpensive and space-saving alternatives to three separate pieces of hardware, but be aware that you risk losing all three components if one fails.

ADDITIONAL HARDWARE

A **scanner** is a hardware device that translates text and illustrations from a hardcopy source into a format that a computer can use. In effect, it "photocopies" an image to your computer. Several types of scanners are available, but a flat-bed scanner is best for document handling. You can use a scanner to add hardcopy photos to a digital photo gallery or scan camera ready art for signage of other printed material.

A **digital camera** stores images on a chip or disk instead of on film. There are many advantages to digital cameras versus film and several disadvantages. One advantage is that most digital cameras allow you to view the photo immediately so that you can take another if the original does not satisfy you. Unwanted images can be deleted instantly. You also have almost immediate access to images using an interface with your computer. Pictures can be added to proposals or sent to clients via e-mail immediately. However, unlike film, the resolution of digital images is limited by the amount of memory the camera has, the optical resolution, and for hardcopies, the resolution of the printer. Even the very best digital camera connected to the best printer cannot produce film-quality prints.

A **CD-R drive** (compact disk-recordable drive) allows you to write data to specially formatted compact disks. More commonly known as a CD burner, this device and its accompanying software will let you store large amounts of data on one disk. A typical CD will hold as much data as 500 floppy disks, making this the ideal storage medium for photo galleries and archiving files. CDs also have a longer life than floppy disks or magnetic tape, making them a possible choice for data backup. Only one CD burner is needed per office, though you will find if you purchase a new personal computer that many now come with a CD-R drive as standard equipment.

Networking

According to searchNetworking.com, in reference to technology, **networking** is the "construction, design, and use of network, including the physical (cabling, hub, bridge, switch, router, and so forth), the selection and use of telecommunication protocol and computer software for using and managing the network, and the establishment of operation policies and procedures related to the network." In plain language, networking is anything related to the network hardware or software, or the rules and regulations for using the network.

Networking is the computer tech pulling wire to install a computer for a new employee. Networking is also a memo from the boss about the procedures for accessing and using files from the server. DMCs use networking internally to manage their physical systems.

Internet

The **Internet** is a global "network of networks" connecting hundreds of millions of computers. Conceived in 1969 to allow research computers at several universities to "talk" to each other, the "Net" now connects more than 100 countries, allowing the exchange of data, news, and opinions. The most widely used portion of the Internet is the World Wide Web, often shortened to WWW or simply "the Web." Using the Web, you have access to millions of pages of information.

The Internet has drastically changed the way DMCs do business. General information can be obtained about clients, venues and suppliers. Industry Web sites and trade publications offer informative and educational information, while CVB Web sites usually include myriad information about a destination, including an event calendar. The Internet lets you access everything from a virtual tour of a prospective venue, to the sunset/sunrise times on a specific date nine months in the future, to maps with directions to a new attraction. Communication, business networking, proposal request, customer service and most aspects of "doing business" can now be done via the Internet.

Web Sites

Just as you might use the Internet to find information about a client or vendor, rest assured that your potential clients are also looking for information about you. A **Web page** is simply a document on the World Wide Web. A **Web site** consists of several or many pages linked together. Your Web site might be the first impression that clients receive of your company. Make sure that it properly projects your company image.

Prior to creating (or having someone else create) your company Web site, consider your goals in terms of marketing impact and services provided. Make sure your Web site is easy to find and easy to navigate. A straightforward Web address is best. Although "www.dmc.com" might seem short and sweet, if your company name is Destination Solutions, the most likely thing a client will type into a Web browser will be www.destinationsolutions.com. Also, flashy graphics and great music are wonderful additions, but if a potential client cannot quickly determine how to contact you, your Web site has not served its main purpose.

Telecommunications

Dictionary.com defines **telecommunication** as, "The science and technology of communication at a distance by electronic transmission of impulses, as by telegraph, cable, telephone, radio, or television." These impulses can be used to deliver data, text, pictures, voice, and video over long distance.

The tools that DMCs use for telecommunication include fax machines, telephones, and cell phones with voice mail (including remote retrieval capabilities), pagers, two-way radios, and more.

Security and System Safety

The establishment of guidelines and protocol to ensure security and privacy is necessary to a modern DMC. **Network security** is the protection of networks and their services from unauthorized modification, destruction, or disclosure, and assurance that the network performs for critical functions. Network security also includes providing for data integrity.

The most basic form of security is **password protection.** Most operating systems require, or at least allow for, establishing a password to gain access to a computer or network. Ideally, a password will be changed on a regular basis and will be a string of characters that is difficult to guess. Unfortunately, most passwords are actually just the user's name or initials, or, worse yet, the word "password." If your company establishes a policy pertaining to passwords and demands that each password be known only by the user and one other person, usually the tech or a management person, your network will be much more secure.

Take extra care when determining a password for a laptop computer that you travel with. Having your laptop lost or stolen could mean more than the loss of a valuable piece of hardware if your data are also in the hands of another person because your password is the same as the name on the business card tucked inside the laptop case.

Another component of network security is a **firewall,** usually a combination of hardware and software that limits access to and from a network. All messages entering or leaving the protected network pass through the firewall, which looks at each message and blocks those that do not meet the specified security criteria. A firewall prevents outsiders from accessing your resources and also controls what outside resources your users can access.

Backup software, mentioned earlier, can also be considered a form of security. Having your data backed up and moved out can protect your company in the event your data are affected by anything from a virus, to a disgruntled employee, to a hard-drive crash, to a leaking water pipe.

In conclusion, you must be aware that technology advances at a pace close to the speed of light. The basic components of hardware and software remain constant, but they continually manifest themselves in the form of new programs and faster, smaller, better systems and peripherals. By the time you read this, today's hot software will be on the bargain shelf and what was brand new in 2002 will be too old and slow for your grandmother.

Key Ideas

Dramatic changes in technology have affected the way business is conducted. Like any other business, destination management companies must keep abreast of the latest advances to better serve their clients.

Software refers to the instructions that make a computer function. There are two basic types of software—systems software, which includes the operating system, and utilities and applications software. Types of applications software include word processing, spreadsheet, e-mail, antivirus, database, room diagramming, photo editing, online registration, and backup software.

Hardware is the physical computer equipment including cables, connectors, power supply, and peripherals. Personal computers service one user. Servers manage network resources for multiple users. Additional hardware includes, but is not limited to, printers, scanners, digital cameras, and CD-R drives.

The Internet is a global network connecting hundreds of millions of computers, with the World Wide Web being the most widely used portion. A Web site consists of several Web pages that can be accessed using the Web.

Ensuring privacy and network security is a necessity. Password protection is the most basic form of security. Firewalls use a combination of hardware and software to limit access to and from a network.

Key Questions

1. What is the difference between hardware and software? Name three examples of each.
2. What software will help you most increase productivity and why?
3. Why should a DMC have a Web site?
4. How does effective technology utilization add credibility to your organization?

Key Terms

antivirus software
applications software
backup software
CD-R drive
client/server environment
database software
desktop publishing
digital camera
e-mail
e-vite
field
file
firewall
hardware
Internet
intranet
networking

network security
online registration software
password protection
PC
personal computer
photo-editing software
record
room-diagramming software
scanner
software
spreadsheet
systems software
Technology Revolution
telecommunication
Web page
Web site
word processing

CHAPTER 12

Risk Management

"I usually sum up risk management by saying, 'Hope for the best. . . . Plan for the worst.' The related follow-up we share with clients is, 'It's easier (and cheaper) to KEEP you out of trouble than to GET you out of trouble!' "

BARBARA F. DUNN, ESQ.

ATTORNEY AND PARTNER

HOWE & HUTTON, LTD.

IN THIS CHAPTER YOU WILL LEARN HOW TO:

- Identify and understand "risks" within the destination management industry.
- Understand the meaning of risk management.
- Realize the risks and hazards in everyday destination management.
- Recognize the responsibility of risk management and the risk services.
- Understand how insurance affects risks and hazards.
- Identify various types of insurance.
- Know the risk options.
- Protect a business as an owner.
- Identify liability criteria for selecting a destination management company.

U.S. Society today is particularly litigious. Because of the increased potential risks and dangers at programs, businesses are developing new security and safety compliances and integrating these rules and methods into their business model.

Identifying and understanding *risks* in today's destination management industry is paramount to the success of any program. Risk management should be as much a part of the overall program guidelines as research, planning, budget, and evaluation.

What is **risk management?** It is recognizing the chance of injury, damage or loss, a gamble, or a hazard and having responsibility for or/and a means to prevent it.

Destination management is an industry that plans and produces activities that are expected to put people in a safe environment with no risks to their safety or personal loss. DMCs accept this responsibility when they sign a contract. Attendees also accept responsibilities by using good judgment when they agree to participate in the activity. It becomes a mutual consent of liability.

Despite all efforts to ensure a risk-free environment, incidents do occur. Before the program, it is the responsibility of the servicing DMC to review all possible risks involved in all activities and consider and correctly address each risk.

Legal Issues

Destination management companies must have a basic knowledge of all legal issues that are relevant to their business practice. This knowledge ensures and protects their own interests, as well as their client's and their own financial investments. Managing any type of program requires a great amount of legal knowledge. Without proper protection, risks are unnecessarily established.

The first step in program planning is making the **offer,** or the *proposal.* According to Sherri Bennett of Martindale–Hubbell, an offer must be communicated to another person; it remains open until it is accepted or rejected. Some terms of an offer, like price, quantity, and description, must be specific and definite because the offer has to identify the basic obligation of the contract.

Acceptance is an acknowledgment by the person to whom the offer was made that the offer is accepted. The acceptance must comply with the terms of the offer and must be communicated to the person who proposed the deal. **Consideration** is the bargained-for exchange.

Besides the fundamental elements of a contract (offer, acceptance, and consideration), there are other requirements: competence, consent, and legality.

Competence to make a contract means the legal capacity to make a contract. **Consent** means that each party to the contract must agree to the terms of the contract. **Legality** refers to the obligations, rights, and liabilities of contracts. It is imperative that DMCs understand that a legally binding document is fair to both parties, is understood by both parties, and covers all legal issues. A negotiated contract is a contract resulting from dickering over the terms of the agreement. The parties of a truly negotiated contract have these characteristics:

- They bargain for the terms.
- They know and understand the provisions.
- They consent to all provisions.

Contracts are everywhere. They are a part of modern life, and we enter into them, and perform them, every day. They are necessary to the acquisition of goods and services in the marketplace. See Appendix 10 for an outline of the contract process.

Insurance

By definition, **insurance** is an agreement or arrangement that shifts the risk of loss from the insured to another party, usually an insurance company. Insurance protects persons, property, and business against financial losses from risk that cannot be eluded. Maintaining proper insurance can be the solution. Once you can recognize the nature of the risk, you can begin to plan to control it.

Insurance in the twenty-first century can be complex and confusing. Insurance protection policies within the hospitality industry have come a long way. Today you can insure against everything from rain disruption of an event to program cancellation.

When considering risk insurance, take these things into consideration:

- The potential risks
- Ways to deal with the risks
- When to insure against risk

RISK OPTIONS

Familiarize yourself with the risk options. You may simply avoid the risk altogether, but within the DMC industry, this would be very difficult to do. Another option is to accept the risk. You can try to lessen or get rid of the risk. Or you can move the risk to another party. You can purchase insurance.

Once you have identified the risk options, you should contact a reputable insurance company that is familiar with hospitality issues. The insurance industry is composed of more than 6,000 companies representing more than $2.5 trillion in assets. This offers every opportunity to select a company that will work with you and become familiar with common risks. Remember that every risk is potentially insurable.

COMMON INSURANCE—WHO NEEDS IT?

The following terms are insurance definitions that are relative to providing risk management in the destination management industry. **Casualty insurance** was originally created to protect against loss or liability caused by accidents, but in the contemporary program management industry, it now covers all risks not included in property insurance. **Coinsurance** is the sharing of expenses between the insurance company and the insured. Many times clients, venues, entertainment, and so on will be included on insurance policies as the coinsured.

Competent parties are people capable of entering into a contract. In many states, age and mental competency are named as exclusions as competent parties. Exclusion is also defined as a condition or result not covered by an insurance policy, and clearly spelled out in the contract.

Trying to understand the consequences or **hazards,** conditions that increase the likelihood that a loss will be more severe, generally leads to need for liability insurance. **Moral hazards** are caused by the indifference or laziness of someone such that the likelihood of a loss is increased. **Physical hazards** are specific, tangible conditions that increase the likelihood that a loss will be greater in severity. **Liability insurance** is insurance that protects you in the event that you carelessly cause bodily injury or property damage to other people. The liability can be because of negligence or a failure to live up to the promises made under a contract.

Because destination management companies often place attendees on water vessels, yachts, cruise ships, or barges, **Marine insurance**—insurance coverage related to protection on or around water—is necessary.

You should also understand the following terms and incorporate them if necessary:

Additional insured is an individual or organization listed as covered by a primary insurance agreement. It is also informally referred to as coinsured. **All-risk coverage** is property insurance covering losses arising from any fortuitous cause, except those that are specifically excluded. **Cancellation insurance** is a policy that protects the financial interest of the event sponsor or event organizer in the event of a cancellation.

A **certificate of insurance** is not insurance coverage, but merely serves as written evidence of insurance, while **indemnification** is insurance protection from a loss under stated circumstances or a reimbursement for liabilities. A **security bond** is a promise by one party to be liable to a third party for the debt or obligation of a second party. Risk is not impacted: rather, it becomes someone else's responsibility.

Commercial general liability is a broad form of liability insurance providing protection from liability claims for bodily injury and property damage resulting from the use of products or services, or completed operations, excluding automobile liability. **Comprehensive general public liability insurance** is an umbrella insurance policy that the event manager or event sponsor must maintain in full force to cover injuries, fire, theft, and other potential liabilities. It covers lawsuits brought forth by event participants. **Financial responsibility law** is a statutory provision requiring owners of automobiles to provide evidence of their ability to pay damages arising out of automobile operations.

Protecting Your Business

Every destination management company should ensure protection and security systems that make a comprehensive package for essential business. DMCs should not limit their risk assessment to what they see themselves. Entrepreneurs are encouraged to have at least two insurance agents conduct their own risk management within the business. Although business needs vary widely from one DMC to another, a necessary checklist of policies must be considered to include the following:

- **Business owner coverage:** Otherwise known as *catch-all* coverage, business owner insurance provides damage protection from fire and other miscellaneous coverage and also offers a degree of liability protection.
- **Property insurance:** This can augment the property coverage offered by business owner insurance. Property insurance covers damage to the building that houses your business, as well as the contents:
  - The building (if other than your own home) in which you do business
  - The fixtures utilized to run the business (fixed racks, commercial stoves, etc.)
  - Contents used in your business, including computers, forms, inventory, and stock
- **Liability insurance:** This may be the most important insurance business owners can get. This covers damage to property or injuries suffered by someone else for which you are held responsible. It is important to point out that you can be held liable for the actions of people acting on your behalf, paid or volunteer, under the **doctrine of respondent superior.** Under this doctrine, the business (the master) can be held vicariously liable for its employees' (servants or agents) misdeeds if the employees are operating within the scope of their duties. This can take in a range of disasters, from the attendee who trips on a tour to the guest who burns himself on coffee served at an event.
- **Product liability insurance:** This insurance is necessary if you make a product that could conceivably harm someone else. For instance, a catering business might worry about serving spoiled meat.
- **Errors and omissions insurance:** This coverage is particularly important for service-based businesses, offering protection should you make a mistake that causes a customer some harm.
- **Business income insurance:** This is disability coverage for your business that ensures you get paid if you lose income as a result of damage that shuts down or limits your business.

- **Automobile insurance:** Businesses that use cars or trucks in some manner should have this type of insurance for collision and liability coverage. This can include the following:
  - Collision
  - Comprehensive
  - Rental
  - Towing coverage for the automobiles owned by the business

Even though this list is daunting, entrepreneurs should never settle for inadequate insurance.

Common Risks Associated with Destination Management

As with any niche industry, there are certain risks that are commonplace and shared within destination management. DMCs are responsible for putting people on buses, boats, trains, and all other types of vehicles. They also plan and organize events with food and beverage, entertainment and décor. With each and every planned activity comes the chance of injury, damage, or loss.

Destination management companies protect their attendees and themselves by recognizing each potential risk, minimizing the risk as much as possible, and purchasing the appropriate insurance to ensure safety and security. See Figure 12-1 for risks that may be associated with the destination management industry.

What You Should Know Before Choosing a DMC

When it comes to attendee safety and security, clients should carefully screen destination management companies based on their risk management program. When DMCs effectively integrate risk management with business strategies, they prove themselves to be professional, successful, and worthy to their customers. Destination management companies should provide customers with a

Activity	Risk
Adventure tours	Falling, drowning, accidents
Cars/limos	Auto accidents, falling
Charter air flights	Accidents, food poisoning, plane no-shows
Cruise/yachts	Illness, food poisoning, accidents, itinerary changes
Décor/props	Falling props or debris, personal injury
Entertainers	Cancellation, inappropriate material
Fireworks/pyrotechnics	Fire, smoke, debris, hearing damage
Food and beverage	Food poisoning, allergic reactions, intoxicated guests
Helicopter tours	Accidents, motion illness
Hot-air balloons	Accidents, fire
Jeep tours	Accidents
Liquor service	Drinking and driving after function, personal injury, injury to others, damage to property
Mopeds/scooters	Accidents
Parasailing	Personal injury
Sporting activities	Personal injury, injury to others
Teambuilding activities	Personal injury, injury to others
Tour buses	Accidents, falling, personal injury
Water sports	Personal injury, injury to others, accidents
Whitewater rafting	Accidents, personal injury, drowning
Youth care/programs	Personal injury, kidnapping, lost child, abuse

Figure 12-1
Risks Associated with Destination Management

benchmark for identifying, assessing, monitoring, and managing and controlling program liability issues.

For increased protection from liability, make sure that your vendors (DMCs) provide you with certificates of insurance documenting their levels of coverage. Take the time to learn the language of the liability to protect yourself and the organization you represent.

Make sure to read the vendor's indemnification clause; one party agrees to hold harmless the other party in any claims that may arise against them. You may ask to be named as an additional insured on the vendor's policies that will grant you the same coverage.

Risk Management Case Studies

THE DIFFICULT COMEDIAN

A mega telecommunications company wanted to use a famous comedian for a national sales meeting. The comedian was known for his rude behavior and discriminatory remarks. The client insisted that this entertainer be hired and that the company would protect itself by doing a thorough legal disclaimer outlining what the comedian could and could not say in front of the group. The legal document was nine pages long and was signed by the comedian and his agent and was, of course, co-signed by the client. The DMC's responsibility was to make sure that all logistics were managed for the comedian and his entourage, as well as setting up the green room (talent preparation area). The on-site DMC program manager was given a copy of the client/comedian contract. After the comedian was introduced, he proceeded to say and do everything that he agreed not to say and do. Fortunately for the DMC, there were no legal ramifications, and the client did not take any legal action against the comedian.

THE OFFENDED ATTENDEE

A large pharmaceutical sales meeting was held in a southern state in the United States. The pharmaceutical company asked the local destination management company to buy out a local, famous piano bar, renowned for selecting customer business cards and writing short songs about the person. One of the salesperson's cards was selected and the band proceeded to make up a song about the person. Three weeks after the event, the salesperson filed a legal suit against her company, the company meeting planner, the company human resources director, and the bar, citing sexual harassment. The DMC was not named in the suit, but could very easily have been named as part of the offending party. The suit settled in favor of the salesperson and she was awarded three million dollars. The bar closed.

A SAFER ROAD TO TRAVEL

At an incentive program held on a beautiful island, the client requested that the destination management company arrange for mopeds (light, low-powered motorbikes) to be made available to any guests who might want to use them. The DMC refused, citing company policy prohibiting them from utilizing mopeds, as they had been identified as a high-risk activity. The company planner made arrangements herself, in the name of her company. During a three-day program, there were five accidents involving guests, one resulting in a serious injury to the vice-president of the company. The planner was later fired and the DMC was commended for the warning regarding the risk and danger of mopeds.

RAIN, RAIN, GO AWAY

During a local city tour, a heavy downpour erupted. The group on tour included a military reunion group where the average age was between 75 and 85. While disembarking the bus at one of the stops, an attendee slipped on wet steps and fell onto the street. The DMC and the bus company made every effort to prep the steps and stepping stool by using a towel to dry wet spots. After the accident, all typical safety procedures were followed. An ambulance was immediately called, and all accident and incident reports were filed. The attendee had fractured his elbow and filed a lawsuit within a month after the tour. The case was later settled out of court.

In conclusion, if you think there are a lot of risks and a lot of terms and definitions to remember, you are correct. Risk management and insurance are complicated issues, so let's wrap up this topic with two more terms: insurance agent and lawyer. Make sure you have good relationships with both.

Key Ideas

Identifying and understanding risks in today's destination management is a key component to a safe and successful program. It has been marked as a speculative and high-risk industry. Despite efforts to ensure risk-free programs, incidents do occur. Under standing and applying efforts to protect all are necessary. Various types of insurance shift the risks of loss and liability, and these precautions should be carefully investigated with insurance professionals.

Key Questions

1. Define risk management and its impact on the destination management industry.
2. What potential risks might a destination management company encounter?
3. Define insurance.
4. How does insurance interact with risks and hazards?
5. What are the risk options?
6. What type of insurance would you need for a dinner cruise for 100 corporate guests?
7. List three liability criteria necessary when selecting a destination management company.

Key Terms

acceptance
additional insured
all-risk coverage
automobile insurance
business income insurance
business owner coverage
cancellation insurance
casualty insurance
certificate of insurance
coinsurance
commercial general liability
competence
competent parties
comprehensive general
    public liability insurance
consent
consideration

doctrine of respondent
    superior
errors and omissions insurance
financial responsibility law
hazard
indemnification
insurance
liability insurance
marine insurance
moral hazard
offer
physical hazard
product liability insurance
property insurance
risk management
security bond

CHAPTER 13

Ethics

"Ethical business practices are critical for the longevity of a destination management company. Market research shows that most RFPs are awarded to a DMC based on referrals and reputation. Due to the small universe in which DMCs revolve, the ethical business standards and integrity of the company soon become known to the hospitality industry. Basically, clients do business with people they trust."

HELEN L. MOSKOVITZ, DMCP

EXECUTIVE VICE PRESIDENT

THE KEY EVENT & HELEN MOSKOVITZ GROUP

IN THIS CHAPTER YOU WILL LEARN HOW TO:

- Define ethics.
- Recognize the ethics code of the Association of Destination Management Executives and realize that the association closely monitors these principles.
- Understand the code of ethics that exists within the destination management industry.
- Appreciate the areas that might be considered unethical.
- Recognize business ethics and the benefits of a strong ethics policy.

The principle of ethics can be illustrated by a quote from General H. Norman Schwarzkopf: "The truth of the matter is that you always know the right thing to do. The hard part is doing it."

The Association of Destination Management Executives has adopted the following principles of professional and ethical conduct.

As a member of the Association of Destination Management Executives, I will:

1. Deal with clients, business associates, and suppliers in a professional, businesslike manner.

2. Protect the confidentiality of all proposals and pricing received from suppliers.
3. Provide the supplier with business reasons why the proposal was rejected.
4. Honor signed contracts in spirit as well as intent.
5. Indicate to suppliers whether the program is firm, or if other options/venues are still being considered and any changes in size of group as that information becomes available.
6. Provide host hotel/venue with pertinent information that will directly impact the operation of said hotel/venue.
7. Not use my position in ADME to the detriment or disadvantage of my professional organization, and I will advise all parties, including my organization, of any circumstances that may have the appearance of a conflict of interest.

Ethics and Social Responsibility

Despite alleged breaches of ethical standards, most businesspeople do follow ethical practices. Many destination management companies and industry associations now offer ethics training to their employees and members. Most organizational mission statements include pledges to protect their business environment, contribute to their clients' way of doing business, and improve customer service through integrity. These programs provide benefits such as better customer relationships, loyalty, marketplace success, and improved customer satisfaction ratings. Technology has added a new dimension, leading organizations to do the right thing.

Because ethics and social responsibility are vital topics to all organizations, this book includes an ethics quiz. Go to Appendix 11 to see how you do.

Organizational Behavior

Organizational behavior is the study of what people think, feel, and do in and around organizations. **Organizations** are groups of people who work interdependently toward some purpose. They consist of people who interact with each other to achieve a set of goals. Most organizations want to influence the environment in which they work. Since the pace of change is accelerating and constant transformation is taking place in the work force, values and ethics should receive a lot more attention than in the past.

Organizations should encourage the highest standards of behavior and publish best ethical practices. They can achieve this by raising awareness of issues with employees to help them to build relationships of trust with their customers, other employees, suppliers, administration, and communities in which they work.

The Language of Ethics

Business ethics means more than deciding whether to take home the paperclips. Doing the right thing is not always easy, and pressure to produce and succeed can easily steer one in the wrong direction. Understanding the difference in business ethics language is the first step in designing good business practice.

Values represent stable, long-lasting beliefs about what is important in a variety of situations. They are evaluative standards that help us define what is right and wrong. **Ethics** refers to the moral principles or values that determine whether actions are right or wrong and outcomes are good or bad. **Morals** are the principles or standards with respect to right or wrong in conduct. **Integrity** is a complete, whole, unimpaired condition based on honesty and sincerity.

There is always the fine line of defining the difference among ethics, morals, and the law. The commonality of these terms is that they represent the basis of right versus wrong choices. What is called for is a review of the facts and a thorough determination of the consequences of each possible course of action.

Business Ethics

Managing ethics in the workplace provides tremendous benefits for organizations, its leaders and managers, both morally and practically. This is particularly true today, when it is critical to comprehend and manage highly diverse values in the work setting.

The problem of unsatisfactory involvement of leaders and managers is the lack of discussion and literature about business ethics. They require more practical information about managing ethics, especially about organizational ethics programs and codes of ethics. Organizations must actually put ethical goals and theories into practical actions. A lack of involvement from leaders and managers has produced a great deal of confusion and misunderstanding about business ethics.

WHAT IS BUSINESS ETHICS?

Business ethics is coming to know what is right or wrong in the workplace and doing what's right—in regard to effects of products/services and in relationships with customers. In times of fundamental change, values are no longer followed. Hence, there is no clear moral compass to guide leaders through complex dilemmas about what is right and what is wrong. Most employees believe that business ethics is simply doing the right thing, such as "be good" or "don't lie," and employees don't take business ethics seriously. During times of duress, principles can go right out of the door. As a result, business ethics can be strong preventative medicine.

AREAS OF BUSINESS ETHICS

The first area of business ethics is referred to as **managerial mischief.** Peter Madsen and Jay Shafritz, in their book *Essentials of Business Ethics* (Penguin Books, 1990), further explain that managerial mischief includes "illegal, unethical, or questionable practices of individual managers or organizations, as well as the causes of such behaviors and remedies to eradicate them."

The other broad area of business ethics is **moral mazes** of management, and includes the numerous ethical problems that managers must deal with on a daily basis, such as potential conflicts of interest, wrongful use of resources, mismanagement of contracts, agreements, and so on.

Ninety percent of business schools now provide some form of training in business ethics. Ethics in the workplace can be managed through the use of codes of ethics, codes of conduct, roles of ethicists and ethics committees, policies and procedures, procedures to resolve ethical dilemmas, and ethics training.

BENEFITS OF MANAGING ETHICS IN THE WORKPLACE

The benefits of managing ethics in the workplace are numerous. Attention to business ethics can improve society as a whole, and ethics programs can maintain a moral course in difficult times. Ethics programs nurture strong teamwork and productivity and support employee growth, retention and meaning.

Ethics programs are an insurance policy; they help ensure that policies and procedures are legal. Such programs can help avoid criminal "acts of omission" and can lower fines if problems do occur. Ethics programs help manage values associated with quality management, strategic planning and diversity management, and, most important, formal attention to business ethics is simply the right thing to do.

Mark Pastin, in *The Hard Problems of Management: Gaining the Ethics Edge* (Jossey–Bass, 1986), provides the following four principles for highly ethical organizations:

1. They are at ease interacting with diverse internal and external stakeholder groups. The ground rules of these firms make the good of these stakeholder groups part of the organizations' own good.
2. They are obsessed with fairness. Their ground rules emphasize that the other persons' interests count as much as their own.
3. Responsibility is individual rather than collective, with individuals assuming personal responsibility for actions of the organization. These organizations' ground rules mandate that individuals are responsible to themselves.
4. They see their activities in terms of purpose. This purpose is a way of operating that members of the organization highly value. And purpose ties the organization to its environment.

Organizations should recognize that managing ethics is a process and the bottom line of an ethics program is accomplishing preferred behaviors in the workplace.

Technology

Information technology has created a new way of doing business. With this technology revolution comes the added responsibility of business protocol and rules. It appears that everything today is electronic: communications, proposals, service agreements, entertainment, marketing, accounting, venue procurement, virtual site visits, and all business in general. Although some might argue that traditional ways of doing business will prevail, the majority of successful businesses embrace electronic commerce and enhance the traditional systems that they have.

What is computer and technology ethics? The following is excerpted from an article that first appeared in Terrell Ward Bynum, ed., *Computers & Ethics*, Blackwell, 1985 (a special issue of the journal *Metaphilosophy*).

> *"Computers are special technology and they raise some special ethical issues. . . .* **Computer ethics** *is the analysis of the nature and social impact of computer technology and the corresponding formulation and justification of policies for the ethical use of such technology. A typical problem in computer ethics arises because there is a policy vacuum about how computer technology should be used. Computers and technology information provide us with many new capabilities, and these, in turn, give us new choices for action. Often, either no policies for conduct in these situations exist or existing policies seem inadequate. A central task of ethics is to determine what we should do in such cases, i.e., to formulate policies to guide our actions. Some ethical situations confront us as individuals and some as a society. Technology ethics includes consideration of both personal and social policies for the ethical use of technology.*
>
> *Even within a coherent conceptual framework, the formulation of a policy for using technology can be difficult. As we consider different policies we discover something about what we value and what we don't. Because technology provides us with new possibilities for acting, new values emerge."*

Even electronic communication needs to be standardized, as words and symbols can send expressive and emotional messages that can be misinterpreted. See Figure 13-1 for suggestions on e-mail protocol.

As with any social economic situation, organizations should seek expert advice in setting technology protocol and offer continuous staff training on rules and regulations.

- DO write a clear, concise subject line for every message. E-mail without a subject line is hard for recipients to categorize and, as result, may not get the attention it deserves.
- DON'T attach files to your messages unless you've confirmed in advance the recipient will be able to easily download and open the attachments. Unsolicited attachments can anger recipients because they bog down the process of collecting new mail and hog hard disk space.
- DO check your inbox regularly if you're giving your e-mail address to business contacts. It is difficult to carry on an e-mail conversation with people who only collect their messages twice a month.
- DON'T write messages entirely in capital letters. IT'S THE E-MAIL EQUIVALENT OF SHOUTING AND IS VERY RUDE.
- DO use correct grammar and spelling in all messages, and always sign your full name at the bottom of the message.
- DON'T engage in "flame wars," the Internet term for volleys of nasty or insulting messages. If you receive flames, ignore them. To protect yourself from accidentally getting flamed, avoid subtle humor and sarcasm that can be easily misinterpreted given e-mail's inherent lack of social or emotional context.
- DO pick up the telephone and make a call if the information you need to convey is critical.
- DON'T send a message to a long list of recipients who don't need to hear from you, or sign up others for a regular mailing list without first getting their permission. Also, double check the address on responses to group mailings to make sure you're replying only to the author, not the entire group.
- DO learn about the "blind carbon copy" feature in your e-mail software, which hides the recipient list, and use this feature when sending messages to large groups. No one likes to receive e-mail that begins with several screens full of recipient names.
- DON'T pass along chain letters, even if you're risking several thousand years of bad luck. E-mail chain letters are both illegal and annoying.
- DO show restraint in quoting from the original message when sending a reply.
- DON'T create a big "signature" for the bottom of every outgoing message, cluttered with the wisdom of your favorite philosopher or too-cute drawings made from letters of the alphabet. A signature should be no more than five lines, with limited basics such as your name, job title, and address and phone number.

Figure 13-1
Suggestions for E-mail Protocol
Copyright ©2000 San Jose Mercury News. All rights reserved.
Reproduced with permission

Best Business Practices

To maintain the best business practices, establish interpersonal determinants of business behavior. Understand every client's needs and motives, recognize legitimate business opportunities, and understand perceptions and attitudes.

Diligent customer business-to-business research will provide the necessary information on demographic customer type, end-use application, and purchasing situations. DMCs' business tools set the standards for their good business practices, and customer behavior, product strategy, logistics management, physical fulfillment, promotional strategy, personal selling and sales force management, pricing strategy, risk management, and customer satisfaction ratings or evaluations should be part of the tool box for their organizational environment. Demonstrating and delivering a stable business plan will create good ethical business practices. From risk assessment to administration, doing business ethically makes for better business. Integrity powers business ethics.

Using Agreements to Guard Against Unethical Behavior

Put everything in writing to substantiate the agreement between you and the client, or you and the supplier. The line between acceptable and unethical behavior is not always clear.

These behaviors are considered unethical:

- Knowingly interfering with the legal and contractual rights of others
- Knowingly reproducing a program designed by a competitor
- Accepting a supplier's gift in exchange for business not in the best interest of the client

Regarding gifts from suppliers, the barometer for this fine line is, "Would you feel comfortable if your acceptance of the gift became public knowledge?" (If you make a decision in hopes that no one will find out, chances are that the decision is not ethical.)

Proposals—Protecting Intellectual Property

As more and more meeting and event professionals emerge, it has become imperative to train and teach good standards and ethics. Many people do not realize that destination management is much like any profession and should be treated as such. Architects and professional designers, attorneys, and so on charge for time and materials. Destination management companies typically do not charge for services during the proposal stage. Therefore, it is imperative for DMCs to protect their intellectual property as best they can. MAC Meetings and Events in St. Louis, Missouri, uses various ways to protect intellectual property.

Every proposal is copyrighted, and the following is stated on the front of proposals:

CREATIVE PROPERTY

*All ideas and concepts detailed in the enclosed proposal have been developed exclusively by MAC Meetings and Events, LLC for **Client, M/Y,** and are considered by MAC Meetings and Events to be of a proprietary nature. These ideas and concepts remain the property of MAC.*

*In this respect, **Client** must honor our proprietary rights to the content of this proposal and refrain from disclosing its contents to our competitors or any third party. Unauthorized use of these ideas and concepts is strictly prohibited.*

All documents, written proposals and other materials submitted by MAC Meetings and Events shall be returned to MAC upon request.

Should you wish to produce the ideas and concepts included in this proposal without retaining MAC Meetings and Events, a consultation FEE of $1,000.00 will be required.

When meeting to discuss proprietary information with clients, MAC Meetings and Events has the client sign a nondisclosure document.

When Rights Go Wrong

Within the destination management industry it is not uncommon for clients and competitors to abuse common rights of protection. There are clients that request multiple bids from companies asking for detailed descriptions of themed events, food and beverage, unique venues, sample entertainment, floor plans, renderings, and other components of programs, only to capture their ideas. The client then contacts all vendors and venues directly, circumventing the DMC. The DMC loses a considerable amount of money on time and materials spent developing ideas for the client. This unethical strategy can only be corrected if and when destination management companies unite and begin to charge for proposals and ideas.

At times, an organization might require its in-house planner to get three bids or more for DMC services. Some planners ultimately intend to use the incumbent supplier or favorite vendor, but still put DMCs through the arduous task of preparing and submitting proposals. A destination company must ascertain, before preparing a proposal for clients, how many proposals are being accepted, criteria for acceptance, if the incumbent company is bidding on the program, and the client's decision timeline. It still might be difficult to know if the client's response is sincere.

Another blatant unethical behavior is when a competitive destination management company obtains another DMC's proposal, copies the creative ideas, and undercuts the cost of services.

Through destination management consortiums and associations like the Association of Destination Management Executives, DMCs are sharing questionable behavior of clients, and common client abusers are being identified. DMCs are banding together to reject Request for Proposal (RFP) and Request for Information (RFI) from these habitual good practice violators. In recent cases, one renowned destination management company sent a bill to the client for time and materials on a rejected proposal, and in another case, a DMC reported the planner to the company department manager.

Unethical practice by one DMC to another DMC is monitored and policed by industry organizations, which have systems in place to accept and review unethical charges with repercussions of penalties, including expulsion from industry organizations.

An Ethical Dilemma and Possible Solution

An individual calls a local DMC and requests a proposal, including several options, for an off-site event for 500+ guests. The contact identifies herself as a "planner" from "an independent meeting planning firm" and explains that the firm is planning a one-night, off-site event for XYZ Corporation (a Fortune 100 company) one month from today.

When the sales manager from the DMC asks specific qualifying questions, the planner is forthcoming with all demographic information about the group, history on when and where the event has taken place in past years, and feedback on initial themes presented by the DMC. The planner is evasive when asked about the budget for the event, replying with, "We just want to see what you can come up with at this point." She states that the firm needs the proposal within one week, and that it wants to come out for a site inspection the following week, without the client, to "narrow down the top two or three choices."

So, the DMC spends the next few days researching and developing several original themes and ideas, gathering information from vendors, placing venues on hold, and preparing for the site inspection. By week's end, after investing hundreds of person-hours, the proposal is creatively packaged and express-mailed to the planner.

The following week, the DMC conducts the site inspection, as requested, with the planner and two of the planner's associates for a two-day site inspection to view, taste, and evaluate the proposed venues and themes. At the end of the site inspection, the planner requests several revisions to three of the original proposal themes and gives the DMC less than a week to resubmit the proposal for the planner's (and the planner's client's) review. All the while, the DMC asks for guidance or feedback from the planner regarding the budget, only to receive more ambiguous answers, such as, "I want to see what you come up with." So the DMC invests several more person-hours in completing the requested revisions, reshuffling priorities, and submitting the "final" draft of the proposal to the planner on time.

After several days of unanswered calls and e-mails to the planner, the DMC receives a phone call from its contact at one of the venues it proposed for this event. The contact says that the planner recently contacted the venue directly to place a hold on the same night that the DMC was holding, and that the planner requested menus containing the same items that the DMC had proposed to the planner earlier in the month.

Discouraged, the DMC leaves a long voice mail for the planner, expressing concern over the fact that the planner hasn't returned any of the DMC calls, and recapping the call that the DMC received from its contact at one of the venues it had proposed. The DMC also instructs/requests that the venue maintain the DMC's "first hold" on the venue for the event date, and that the vendor not send the client the same menus (or prices) that were developed by the DMC. The vendor expresses that it doesn't want to "get in the middle of anything" and is inclined to send the planner the requested information.

The DMC expresses that it is unethical for the client to "use" the DMC to identify the venue, create the menus, conduct the site inspection, revise and refine the event logistics, and then attempt to "go direct" to the venue once the program has been designed, in an attempt to avoid contracting and paying the DMC for its services.

The DMC also reminds the vendor that it brings volume business to the venue, and has done so over many years, and that the DMC is one of the primary marketers of the venue for groups. This planner most likely represents only one or two potential events at the venue, every few years!

Eventually, the vendor develops the ethical (and financial) sense to send the planner a letter to the effect that it would be unethical to send information to the planner that was developed with the DMC. It would further be unethical since it was the DMC that originally contacted the venue about the event, on the planner's behalf, and it was the DMC that conducted the site inspection (with the planner's consent). The vendor's letter concludes by suggesting that the planner contact the DMC directly to resolve any issues that might stand in the way of proceeding with the event as designed and refined by the DMC for the planner.

Key Ideas

Ethics are an important component of every profession, and understanding and recognizing the standards that govern conduct is necessary. There is a thin line among ethics, morals, and the law, and the line is not always clear. Managerial mischief and moral mazes are two types of ethical dilemmas that businesses face today. Establish and stick with best business practices. Not only is it the right thing to do, it also makes good business sense. The increasing use of technology has brought about new ethical issues related to computer use, often without specific policies in place. DMCs should establish best practices that relate to their technology and its use. If possible, get everything in writing from both clients and suppliers. This makes it very clear what is expected from each party and will help avoid many ethical dilemmas. In all cases, ask yourself if you would feel comfortable if your actions became known. If you are doing something in the hopes that no one will find out, it is probably unethical.

Key Questions

1. Define business ethics. What is the responsibility of management in regards to ethics within a company?
2. What is the difference among ethics, morals, and the law?
3. List three situations that might be considered unethical within the destination management industry.
4. List and discuss four benefits of managing ethics in the workplace.

Key Terms

business ethics	moral mazes
computer ethics	morals
ethics	organizational behavior
integrity	organizations
managerial mischief	values

Sample Letter of Intent

Client name (hereinafter "CLIENT") acknowledges that it will contract with DMC to perform services for CLIENT, which will be outlined in the contract forthcoming and submitted to client for approval. In doing so, DMC may be called upon to sign contracts for vendors and, as such, CLIENT may hereby authorize DMC to act as its AGENT in negotiating and contracting for specific services (including, as an example but without limitations, hotel(s), meeting space, meeting management services, events, props, and transportation) on behalf of the CLIENT.

CLIENT further acknowledges and agrees that it will indemnify and hold harmless DMC from any costs, debts, liabilities, judgments and expenses that a vendor may attempt to bring against DMC, while in the performance of its obligation to the CLIENT, in acting as its AGENT, and attempting to fulfill the services/activities of the contract between DMC and the CLIENT.

Authority

The person executing this Letter of Intent represents that he or she has the authority to bind the organization to the commitments made herein, and such action is taken with the full knowledge of the governing body of the organization.

Please return signed agreement by **date**.

Signature_____   _____, agent

Name _____   _____

Title _____   _____

For _____   _____
     CLIENT   DMC

Date _____   _____

Facsimile signatures shall be sufficient unless
one party requires originals.

Account #

Sample courtesy of MAC Meetings and Events, St. Louis, MO

Sample Contract for Services

CLIENT ("Client") hereby engages ABC DMC ("ABC") to arrange for and coordinate the services described in the attached Letter of Confirmation dated **CONFIRMATION DATE** ("Services"), addressed to **CLIENT** for the **PROGRAM** program ("Program").

PROJECTED PROGRAM DATES . . . . **DATE**

PROJECTED PROGRAM PRICE . . . . **AMOUNT**

SCHEDULE OF DEPOSITS:

Initial Deposit: **DEPOSIT AMOUNT**   Due Date: **DEPOSIT DUE DATE**
Second Deposit: **DEPOSIT AMOUNT**   Due Date: **DEPOSIT DUE DATE**

Prices for services are detailed in the attached letter of confirmation.
All prices and services are tentative until this contract is signed and dated by both parties.
ABC may declare this contract null and void if it is not signed and returned by client on or before **RETURN-BY DATE.**

Terms and conditions on the back hereof are made part of this contract.

FOR: **CLIENT**
BY: **CONTACT NAME**

Signature: _____   Date:_____

FOR: ABC DMC
BY: **SALES MANAGER,** sales manager

Signature: _____   Date: _____

Program # **ACCOUNT NUMBER**

PLEASE SEND ALL PAYMENTS TO:

ABC DMC
123 Main Street, Suite 1000
Los Angeles, CA 90001

Terms and Conditions

1. **INSURANCE:** ABC carries professional liability insurance covering the rendition of services in connection with this contract. Any additional insurance coverage requested by Client may be provided at additional cost.
2. **PERFORMANCE:** ABC agrees to indemnify and save harmless Client from any costs, debts, liabilities, judgments and expenses for errors or omissions of ABC arising out of or in connection with its performance, as distinguished from the performance or omissions of vendors or suppliers of ABC, under this contract. Client agrees that if a vendor or supplier of ABC causes damage or loss to Client, that such vendor or supplier is solely responsible for compensation and Client waives all rights, causes, or action and claims for indemnity against ABC. Client agrees to hold harmless ABC from liability caused by any act or omission of Client or any employee, member, guest, invitee, of Client, or of any third party of Client, or arising from the use of any facility, equipment, transportation, or other instrumentation used or provided by Client.
3. **PAYMENTS:** Deposits are due and payable according to the Schedule of Deposits on the first page of this Contract for Services. Additional deposits will be required for services added after the Contract for Services is executed. All remaining balances are due and payable as of the invoice date and become delinquent after 21 days. A finance charge of 1.5% per month (APR of 18%) will be charged on any past due amounts.
4. **CANCELLATION:** Should Client cancel all or any part of the services to be rendered by ABC, Client agrees to give prior written

notice of such cancellation to ABC. In such event, Client agrees to pay to ABC the actual costs, including labor, expended or incurred by ABC and the charges of its vendors and suppliers, in connection with the cancelled services, together with a cancellation fee for the canceled services, based on the following schedule:

- Before 60 days prior to program start date = 15% fee
- Between 59 and 22 days prior to program start date = 25% fee
- Between 21 and 15 days prior to program start date = 30% fee
- Within 14 days prior to program start date = 50% fee

5. **ARBITRATION:** ABC shall not be liable for delays caused by Acts of God, civil riot or commotion, strikes, labor disturbance, or causes beyond its reasonable control. In the event a dispute arises, the parties agree to binding arbitration in accordance with the Rules of Arbitration set forth in Code of Civil Procedure Section 1280 and following. The prevailing party in any dispute or to collection action shall be entitled to costs of arbitration, costs of court, and a reasonable attorneys fees and disbursements. The laws of the state of California shall govern this Agreement. Venue shall be in the county of Los Angeles.

6. **HOST LIQUOR:** It is hereby understood and agreed that Client will pay on behalf of ABC all sums which ABC may become obligated to pay as damages because of the liability imposed upon ABC: for bodily injury, sickness or disease, including death at anytime there from, sustained by any person; and for injury to or destruction of any property; resulting from serving of any alcoholic beverage to any employee, member, guest, invitee of Client by ABC.

7. **COPYRIGHT:** Client will be responsible for all copyrights, permits and licenses including BMI/ASCAP. Client agrees to indemnify and hold harmless ABC from any liability caused by any omission of copyrights, permits or licenses in connection with the program.

8. **SURCHARGES:** ABC reserves the right to assess or pass on additional fees, fuel charges, and any other surcharges incurred by ABC or its suppliers in the rendition of services.

Agreed By   Date

Sample courtesy of ACCESS California

Sample Schedule of Services 1

CLIENT: ABC Company
CONTACT: Joe Smith

ACCT #: 2000

CSM: Teri

HOTEL: See assignments below
ACTIVITY: Evening at Aquarium of the Pacific
ACTIVITY DAY/DATE: Friday, September 29, 2004
COACH CO./DRIVER: Guests are walking
FINAL COUNT: approx. 900

Group Information

Managers, directors, and vendors of ABC Company in town for a meeting and promotional campaign lunch. Group is composed of 80 percent male/20 percent female. Attendees are from United States.

COMPANY/CONTACT	PHONE	STAFFING
Teri Home Phone #	————	1. Jane (Westin LB Hotel)
Teri Cell Phone #	————	2. Diane (Renaissance Hotel)
CSM PVT Radio#	836	3. Judy (Hyatt Regency)
		4. Beatriz (LB Hilton)
		5. Carole (Aquarium)
		6. Lillian (Aquarium)

Equipment

SIGNS	BROCHURES	BOX LUNCHES	BEVERAGES	DRIVER GRATS
MAPS	FLOWERS	PAPER GOODS	COOLERS	CO. CHECK
TICKETS	SNACKS	TRASH BAGS	GIFT	

UNIFORM: Casual

Itinerary

STAFF AT HOTELS

ON ARRIVAL: Post yourselves in the lobby and offer walking directions to the Convention Center

7:30 PM   Event officially starts.

8:00 PM   Report to Aquarium registration desk. See Teri for assignment.

10:30 PM   Event ends; staff released.

STAFF AT AQUARIUM

ON ARRIVAL: Please man the registration desk just outside the Aquarium entrance. Guests have a ticket for admission and in-and-out privileges for the evening.

8:00 PM   Teri will meet you at the registration desk for the rest of the evening's assignments.

10:30 PM   Event ends; staff released.

Sample courtesy of ACCESS California

Sample Schedule of Services 2

EVENT PROFILE	PROGRAM PROFILE
EVENT DATE	PROGRAM NUMBER
EVENT NAME	GROUP NAME
# OF GUESTS EXPECTED	GROUP CONTACT
GUARANTEE TO VENUE	PROGRAM DATES
VENUE	TOTAL PAX
HOURS	HOTEL / PHONE #
UNIFORM	HOTEL CONTACT
	INCENTIVE COMPANY
	INCENTIVE CO. CONTACT

GROUP PROFILE

RECONFIRM WITH:	VOICEMAIL:	CELL:
PROGRAM LEAD:	VOICEMAIL:	CELL:
EVENT LEAD:	VOICEMAIL:	CELL:

TOUR STAFF	PHONE #	SPOT TIME	SPOT LOCATION	CELL	SCHEDULED RELEASE

TRANSPORTATION COMPANY/CONTACT	DAYTIME PHONE	AFTER-HOURS PHONE	VEHICLE TYPE	SPOT TIME	SCHEDULED RELEASE

TOUR GUIDE FOLLOW-UP
☐ Guide Release Time: ☐ Actual Pax Count:
☐ Driver Release Time: ☐ Driver Grat Paid: ☐ Driver Initials:

EVENT SCHEDULE

Sample courtesy of The Meeting Manager, San Diego, CA

What to Look for When Chartering a Bus

This information is provided by the National Motorcoach Network.

Making the right choice for your group is a snap! It is especially easy when you use this convenient guide to help you through the selection process. The guide is split into three sections. "The Basics" is right up front and is your initial screening guide. "Meeting Your Needs" focuses on the specific needs of your group. "Safety Issues" probes areas usually left untouched—until a problem occurs. By using the guide, you will have taken steps to assure your group of a safe, comfortable, and satisfying travel experience.

The Basics

Tip #1:   Ask how long the company has been in business. Find out when the company was established, and how long it has been offering charter coach service. A long track record is generally desirable.

Tip #2:   Request the company's DOT number. A DOT (Department of Transportation) number is assigned by the U.S. government and is required to operate legally. The DOT number can be used to check the carrier's safety rating (see Tip #3).

Tip #3:   Ask about their DOT Safety Rating. The U.S. Department of Transportation (DOT) issues safety ratings based on the company's accident record and adherence to Federal Motor Carrier Safety Regulations. The highest possible rating is Satisfactory. Other ratings include Conditional, Not Rated, or

Unsatisfactory. Never charter from a company with an unsatisfactory rating.

Tip #4: Request a Certificate of Insurance. Your carrier should supply a Certificate of Insurance. This certificate shows the carrier's levels of insurance and effective policy dates. Accepted levels of insurance call for $1 million to $5 million combined, single-limit liability coverage.

Tip #5: Ask for references. Request and contact references from similar-type groups traveling on similar-type programs. Never charter from a company unwilling to provide references.

Tip #6: Inquire about the size of their fleet. Overall charter fleet size is important. It provides a gauge to the operator's ability to supply alternate vehicles in the event of a mechanical problem, for multi-bus movements, on weekends or during peak seasons. It also provides some insight into the carrier's success.

Tip #7: Ask if the company is available for inspection. You should inspect a carrier personally whenever possible. Inspect the motorcoach equipment, general offices, and garage facilities. You can tell a lot about a company just by looking.

Tip #8: Inquire about the average age of the equipment operated. Vehicles that are more than 10 years old, unless properly maintained on a preventive maintenance basis, can have a greatly diminished reliability factor. Generally speaking, the newer the coach, the fewer the breakdowns.

Tip #9: Determine if the carrier is a full-service company. Does it have its own maintenance facilities? Can it provide a variety of vehicles to meet your special needs? Ask if it helps arrange tours and special services you require.

Meeting Your Needs

Tip #10: Clearly spell out your schedule and what is involved in detail. Be prepared to provide the company with a detailed itinerary for your trip. This information allows the company to quote on your trip accurately. For your safety, driver's hours are limited by federal regulations. In addition, specify if your driver must stay in the same hotel as your group.

Tip #11: Consider your group's special needs, such as the need for a video system, beverage galley, handicapped access, or other equipment.

Tip #12: Ask if video coaches are available. Video-equipped coaches can be a genuine asset. You can view educational videos or movies to help pass the hours. Sports teams can even view game tapes. This is a great way to see your opponent, or review your own performance.

Tip #13: Ask if the carrier is legally licensed to show motion pictures en route. Only carriers licensed by the Motion Picture Association of America may show copyrighted movies. Ask to see a copy of the carrier's MPAA license. (Films rented from a video store are not licensed for public viewing.)

Tip #14: Be a careful shopper. If your organization requires multiple quotations, make sure careful consideration of the other tips are balanced against cost. A decision based solely on price might not be the best value.

Tip #15: Ask who pays for the driver's room. Is the driver's room included in the charter cost? If not, ask if you are responsible for the driver's room.

Tip #16: Determine company policy for extra mileage costs above the contracted amount. Find out the carrier's policy concerning "overage miles" before you select a carrier—not after you get an inflated bill upon your return!

Safety Issues

Tip #17: Ask if the company adheres to Department of Transportation driver regulations. The DOT limits the number of hours a driver can work. A driver is limited to 10 hours of actual driving time. If your itinerary exceeds this limit, ask the company how it plans to handle your group's needs.

Tip #18: Inquire about the company's procedures for on-the-road emergencies. The company should have access to a nationwide reciprocal maintenance agreement that will assure you of prompt servicing of equipment in all regions of the United States.

Tip #19: Ask if the company has a formal drug and alcohol program. Specify that your carrier supply a copy of its written drug and alcohol policy statement. Never charter from a carrier that does not strongly enforce a drug and alcohol-free workplace.

Tip #20: Request a list of qualified CDL drivers. Ask the carrier to submit a list of current qualified drivers. These drivers must have a CDL (commercial driver's license), a DOT driver's file, a current DOT physical examination, approved medical examiner's card, and any other required driver qualification documentation.

APPENDIX 5

Bus Safety

(Excerpted from the American Bus Association Web site)

Regulation and Oversight of Buses

- The U.S. Department of Transportation, Federal Highway Administration, Federal Motor Carrier Safety Administration, and individual state departments of transportation and motor vehicles are the "safety agencies" for the bus and trucking industries in the United States. They help to maintain and regulate a safe environment for passengers traveling by motorcoach. The agencies provide information on motor carriers' safety status online at www.safersys.org.
- Commercial vehicle safety issues in Canada are regulated by Transport Canada and individual provincial agencies.
- The National Safety Council (NSC) is a nongovernmental, public service organization that also helps to educate and influence policy with regards to motor vehicle safety. The NSC is a widely recognized, authoritative source for tracking and maintaining safety statistics in a variety of different areas, including buses and motorcoaches.
- The Federal Motor Carrier Safety Regulations encompass all of the current federal regulations regarding U.S. commercial drivers and bus safety. These regulations can be found in Part 325-Part 399 and Part 40.
- ABA is a member of the Commercial Vehicle Safety Alliance (CVSA), a nonprofit organization of United States, Canadian, and Mexican government agencies and private industry representatives who are dedicated to improving vehicle safety. It serves as a major

focal point for bringing together the perspectives of enforcement agencies, commercial carriers, and other interests to obtain the best possible solutions regarding safety standards, compliance, education, and enforcement.

National Safety Council Statistics

- Data from the National Safety Council and the U.S. Federal Highway Administration Office of Motor Carriers and Highway Safety show that the intercity motorcoach industry is one of the safest modes of transportation and has been consistently for decades.
- According to the National Safety Council, in an average year more than 360 million passenger trips in the United States are taken by intercity bus, totaling 28 billion passenger miles. Actual motorcoach mileage is estimated at about 945 million.

Source: National Safety Council, Accident Facts, Editions 1989 to 1998.

Motorcoach Inspection

The North American Standard Inspection Procedure was developed by the Commercial Vehicle Safety Alliance (CVSA) in order to help ensure compliance with safety regulations and uniform inspection procedures. Through the Motor Carrier Safety Assistance Program (MCSAP), in cooperation with the Federal Highway Administration (FHWA), the states conduct random safety inspections of both buses and drivers to make sure that safety regulations are being followed on our nation's roadways. Motor carriers are subject to one of five different levels of inspection:

- *Level I—North American Standard Inspection:* This is the most complete and thorough of the standardized inspection procedures. It is conducted by three people: a team leader, a rear inspector, and a front inspector. It includes examination of the commercial driver's license (CDL), medical examiner's certificate and waiver, if applicable, a check for alcohol and drugs, driver's record of duty status (logbook) as required, hours of service compliance, seat belt check of driver, and extensive vehicle checks; including measurement of brake performance, tires, steering mechanism, and emergency exits on buses.

- *Level II—Walk-around driver/vehicle inspection:* This covers both driver and vehicle aspects, but it is conducted without inspecting underneath the vehicle. These inspections include examination of the commercial driver's license (CDL), medical examiner's certificate and waiver, if applicable, check for alcohol and drugs, driver's record of duty status (logbook) as required, hours of service compliance, seat belt check of driver, and extensive vehicle checks; including measurement of brake performance, tires, steering mechanism, and emergency exits on the bus.
- *Level III—Driver-only inspection:* This inspection level is primarily a roadway examination of all the driver-related aspects of the North American Standard Inspection Procedure. These inspections include an examination of the commercial driver's license (CDL), medical examiner's certificate and waiver, if applicable, hours of service compliance, seat belt check of driver, and vehicle inspection report.
- *Level IV—Special inspection:* This level includes a one-time examination of a particular item and is normally performed in support of a study or to verify/refute a trend.
- *Level V—Vehicle-only inspection:* This is a performance of each of the vehicle inspection items specified under the North American Standard Inspection Procedure (Level I), without a driver present, usually at a carrier's terminal facility.

U.S. Motor Carrier Regulations

- *Part 374—Passenger Carrier Regulations:* Prohibits discrimination, limits smoking, describes adequate intercity passenger service, and establishes regulations for excess baggage and incidental charter rights.
- *Part 385—Safety Fitness Procedures:* Establishes procedures to determine the safety fitness of motor carriers, assign safety ratings, and to prohibit motor carriers rated as "unsatisfactory" from operating commercial motor vehicles. This part describes how safety ratings are determined, compliance reviews, safety fitness standards, administrative reviews, and how to request a safety rating change based on corrective actions.
- *Part 387—Minimum Levels of Financial Responsibility for Motor Carriers:* Sets minimum levels of insurance that must be maintained by motor carriers of passengers or property.

- *Part 390—General:* Generally, all private motor carriers of property and for-hire motor carriers operating in interstate or foreign commerce are subject to the Federal Motor Carrier Safety Regulations (Parts 390–399). This part establishes the general applicability, definitions, and information for motor carriers.
- *Part 393—Parts and Accessories Necessary for Safe Operation:* Regulations in this part establish standards for commercial motor vehicle hardware. The rules specify requirements for lighting devices, reflectors, and electrical equipment, brakes, glazing and window construction, fuel systems, coupling devices and towing methods, emergency equipment, cargo securement, as well as frames, cab and body components, wheels, steering, and suspension systems.
- *Part 396—Inspection, Repair, and Maintenance:* Establishes that a carrier must regularly inspect, repair, and maintain commercial motor vehicles. This part also includes recordkeeping requirements, as well as prescribing inspector qualifications.

U.S. Driver Qualifications

- *Part 382—Controlled Substances and Alcohol Use and Testing:* Establishes programs designed to prevent crashes and injuries resulting from the misuse of alcohol and controlled substances by drivers of commercial motor vehicles. Sets requirements for drug testing, including pre-employment, post accident, random, reasonable suspicion, return-to-duty and follow-up testing.
- *Part 383—Commercial Driver's License Standards; Requirements and Penalties:* Establishes guidelines for the issuance of commercial vehicle driver's licenses (CDLs). These requirements outline who can obtain a CDL, employer responsibilities, driver disqualifications and penalties, and testing and licensing procedures (including required knowledge and skills test). Other requirements include vehicle groupings; which depend on the size and weight of the vehicles; special endorsements; which are required for drivers of double/triple trailers; passenger vehicles; tank vehicles; or vehicles that are placarded for hazardous materials, and sets procedures for disqualifying unsafe drivers.
- *Part 391—Qualifications of Drivers:* Establishes qualifications for persons who drive commercial motor vehicles. Specifically, the rules in this part describe what a motor carrier must do in order to qualify drivers. Driver qualification requirements include back-

ground and character checks and physical examinations. This part describes files and records that must be maintained by the carrier.

- *Part 392—Driving of Commercial Motor Vehicles:* Establishes the requirements and responsibilities while driving a commercial motor vehicle. The rules specify requirements while driving and while stopped, the use of lighted lamps and reflectors, fueling precautions, and prohibited practices.
- *Part 395—Hours of Service of Drivers:* Establishes maximum driving and on-duty time for drivers. This part also specifies how drivers and carriers must document a driver's hours of service.

    With few exceptions, a driver may drive for 10 hours, and work up to 15 hours (consisting of driving and nondriving duties), before having 8 hours off-duty. A driver may not drive after having been on duty for 70 hours in the past 8 days. Most drivers are required to document their time in a logbook.

Safety Guide for Passengers

The bus industry is one of the safest modes of transportation on the road, with approximately 40,000 motorcoaches operating in North America. Safety is a top priority for all. The motorcoach industry is proud of its safety record, and wants you, the passenger, to know choosing buses means choosing safety. Here's some background information on requirements your operator must meet in order to do business on the roads:

- *Driver standards/Commercial driver's license (CDL):* All U.S. drivers are required to have a valid, current CDL with a "passenger" endorsement. CDLs are only issued after drivers have demonstrated their abilities, through skills and a knowledge test.
- *Operating authority/company inspection:* All carriers operating in the United States are required to have a Department of Transportation (DOT) identification number. With this DOT identification number you can obtain safety information about the carrier by calling (703) 280-4001.
- *DOT safety ratings:* These ratings are based on the results of onsite inspections for the United States conducted by the Federal Motor Carrier Safety Administration in each state. However, due to the volume of carriers, not all have been visited or assigned a rating. If the information on the carrier that you are looking for is not on the SAFER system, this does not mean that the company is an unsafe carrier. It indicates only that the FMCSA has not yet visited that operator.

- *Insurance:* Ask for proof of a valid, current insurance certificate that provides a minimum, in the United States, of $5 million in liability coverage insurance.
- *Vehicle inspection:* Many states and provinces have mandated inspection programs. Call your state or provincial regulatory agency responsible for inspections to learn more about the inspection procedure.
- Look for proof that the vehicle that you will be riding has passed a mechanical inspection within the last year. This inspection certificate is generally in the form of a decal or report displayed on the coach. Ask your operator for more information.
- If a state or province does not require a periodic inspection, you can call the individual motorcoach company to inquire about inspection, bus maintenance and repair, or you can look for a decal issued by the Commercial Vehicle Safety Alliance (CVSA).

APPENDIX 6

Excerpts from the Americans with Disabilities Act of 1990

S. 933

One Hundred First Congress of the United States of America
AT THE SECOND SESSION
Begun and held at the City of Washington on Tuesday, the twenty-third day of January, one thousand nine hundred and ninety

An Act
To establish a clear and comprehensive prohibition of discrimination on the basis of disability.

Subtitle B—Actions Applicable to Public Transportation Provided by Public Entities Considered Discriminatory

Part I—Public Transportation Other Than by Aircraft or Certain Rail Operations

Section 36.310 Transportation Provided by Public Accommodations

Section 36.310 contains specific provisions relating to public accommodations that provide transportation to their clients or customers. This section has been substantially revised in order to coordinate the requirements of this section with the requirements applicable to these transportation systems that will be contained in the regulations issued by the Secretary of Transportation pursuant to section 306 of the ADA, to be codified at 49 CFR part 37. The Department notes that, although the responsibility for issuing regulations applicable to transportation systems operated by public accommodations is divided between this Department and the Department of Transportation, enforcement authority is assigned only to the Department of Justice.

The Department received relatively few comments on this section of the proposed rule. Most of the comments addressed issues that are not specifically addressed in this part, such as the standards for accessible vehicles and the procedure for determining whether equivalent service is provided. Those standards will be contained in the regulation issued by the Department of Transportation. Other commenters raised questions about the types of transportation that will be subject to this section. In response to these inquiries, the Department has revised the list of examples contained in the regulation.

Paragraph (a)(1) states the general rule that covered public accommodations are subject to all of the specific provisions of subparts B, C, and D, except as provided in Sec.36.310. Examples of operations covered by the requirements are listed in paragraph (a)(2). The **stated examples include hotel and motel airport shuttle services, customer shuttle bus services operated by private companies** and shopping centers, student transportation, and shuttle operations of recreational facilities such as stadiums, zoos, amusement parks, and ski resorts. This brief list is not exhaustive. **The section applies to any fixed route or demand responsive transportation system operated by a public accommodation for the benefit of its clients or customers.** The section does not apply to transportation services provided only to employees. Employee transportation will be subject to the regulations issued by the Equal Employment Opportunity Commission to implement title I of the Act. However, if employees and customers or clients are served by the same transportation system, the provisions of this section will apply.

Paragraph (b) specifically provides that a public accommodation shall remove transportation barriers in existing vehicles to the extent that it is readily achievable to do so, but that the installation of hydraulic or other lifts is not required.

Paragraph (c) provides that public accommodations subject to this section shall comply with the requirements for transportation vehicles and systems contained in the regulations issued by the Secretary of Transportation.

ADA Title II: Public Transportation

The transportation provisions of Title II cover public transportation services, such as city buses and public rail transit (e.g. subways, commuter rails, Amtrak). Public transportation authorities may not discriminate against people with disabilities in the provision of their services. They must comply with requirements for accessibility in newly purchased vehicles, make good faith efforts to purchase or lease accessible used buses, remanufacture buses in an accessible manner, **and, unless it would result in an undue burden, provide paratransit where they operate fixed-route bus or rail systems. Paratransit is a service where individuals who are unable to use the regular transit system independently (because of a physical or mental impairment) are picked up and dropped off at their destinations.**

Questions and complaints about public transportation should be directed to:

Federal Transit Administration
U.S. Department of Transportation
400 Seventh Street, S.W.
Washington, D.C. 20590
www.fta.dot.gov/office/civ.htm
(888) 446-4511 (voice/relay)
(202) 366-2285 (voice)
(202) 366-0153 (TTY)

Sec. 221. Definitions

As used in this part:

(1) Demand responsive system.—The term "demand responsive system" means any system of providing designated public transportation which is not a fixed route system.

(2) Designated public transportation.—The term "designated public transportation" means transportation (other than public school transportation) by bus, rail, or any other conveyance (other than transportation by aircraft or intercity or commuter rail transportation (as defined in section 241)) that provides the general public with general or special service (including charter service) on a regular and continuing basis.

(3) Fixed route system.—The term "fixed route system" means a system of providing designated public transportation on which a vehicle is operated along a prescribed route according to a fixed schedule.

(4) Operates.—The term "operates," as used with respect to a fixed route system or demand responsive system, includes operation of such system by a person under a contractual or other arrangement or relationship with a public entity.

(5) Public school transportation.—The term "public school transportation" means transportation by school bus vehicles of school-children, personnel, and equipment to and from a public elementary or secondary school and school-related activities.

(6) Secretary.—The term "Secretary" means the Secretary of Transportation.

Sec. 222. Public Entities Operating Fixed Route Systems

(a) Purchase and Lease of New Vehicles.—It shall be considered discrimination for purposes of section 202 of this Act and section 504 of the Rehabilitation Act of 1973 (29 U.S.C. 794) for a public entity that operates a fixed route system to purchase or lease a new bus, a new rapid rail vehicle, a new light rail vehicle, or any other new vehicle to be used on such system, if the solicitation for such purchase or lease is made after the 30th day following the effective date of this subsection and if such bus, rail vehicle, or other vehicle is not readily accessible to and usable by individuals with disabilities, including individuals who use wheelchairs.

(b) Purchase and Lease of Used Vehicles.—Subject to subsection (c)(1), it shall be considered discrimination for purposes of section 202 of this Act and section 504 of the Rehabilitation Act of 1973 (29 U.S.C. 794) for a public entity which operates a fixed route system to purchase or lease, after the 30th day following the effective date of this subsection, a used vehicle for use on such system unless such entity makes demonstrated good faith efforts to purchase or lease a used vehicle for use on such system that is readily accessible to and usable by individuals with disabilities, including individuals who use wheelchairs.

(c) Remanufactured Vehicles.—

(1) General rule.—Except as provided in paragraph (2), it shall be considered discrimination for purposes of section 202 of this Act and section 504 of the Rehabilitation Act of 1973 (29 U.S.C. 794) for a public entity which operates a fixed route system—

(A) to remanufacture a vehicle for use on such system so as to extend its usable life for 5 years or more, which remanufacture begins (or for which the solicitation is made) after the 30th day following the effective date of this subsection; or

(B) to purchase or lease for use on such system a remanufactured vehicle which has been remanufactured so as to extend its usable life for 5 years or more, which purchase or lease occurs after such 30th day and during the period in which the usable life is extended; unless, after remanufacture, the vehicle is, to the maximum extent feasible, readily accessible to and usable by individuals with disabilities, including individuals who use wheelchairs.

(2) Exception for historic vehicles.—

(A) General rule.—If a public entity operates a fixed route system any segment of which is included on the National Register of Historic Places and if making a vehicle of historic character to be used solely on such segment readily accessible to and usable by individuals with disabilities would significantly alter the historic character of such vehicle, the public entity only has to make (or to purchase or lease a remanufactured vehicle with) those modifications which are necessary to meet the requirements of paragraph (1) and which do not significantly alter the historic character of such vehicle.

(B) Vehicles of historic character defined by regulations.—For purposes of this paragraph and section 228(b), a vehicle of historic character shall be defined by the regulations issued by the Secretary to carry out this subsection.

Sec. 223. Paratransit as a Complement to Fixed Route Service

(a) General Rule.—It shall be considered discrimination for purposes of section 202 of this Act and section 504 of the Rehabilitation Act of 1973 (29 U.S.C. 794) for a public entity which operates a fixed route system

(other than a system which provides solely commuter bus service) to fail to provide with respect to the operations of its fixed route system, in accordance with this section, paratransit and other special transportation services to individuals with disabilities, including individuals who use wheelchairs, that are sufficient to provide to such individuals a level of service (1) which is comparable to the level of designated public transportation services provided to individuals without disabilities using such system; or (2) in the case of response time, which is comparable, to the extent practicable, to the level of designated public transportation services provided to individuals without disabilities using such system.

(b) Issuance of Regulations.—Not later than 1 year after the effective date of this subsection, the Secretary shall issue final regulations to carry out this section.

(c) Required Contents of Regulations.—

(1) Eligible recipients of service.—The regulations issued under this section shall require each public entity which operates a fixed route system to provide the paratransit and other special transportation services required under this section—

(A)(i) to any individual with a disability who is unable, as a result of a physical or mental impairment (including a vision impairment) and without the assistance of another individual (except an operator of a wheelchair lift or other boarding assistance device), to board, ride, or disembark from any vehicle on the system which is readily accessible to and usable by individuals with disabilities; (ii) to any individual with a disability who needs the assistance of a wheelchair lift or other boarding assistance device (and is able with such assistance) to board, ride, and disembark from any vehicle which is readily accessible to and usable by individuals with disabilities if the individual wants to travel on a route on the system during the hours of operation of the system at a time (or within a reasonable period of such time) when such a vehicle is not being used to provide designated public transportation on the route; and (iii) to any individual with a disability who has a specific impairment-related condition which prevents such individual from traveling to a boarding location or from a disembarking location on such system;

(B) to one other individual accompanying the individual with the disability; and

(C) to other individuals, in addition to the one individual described in subparagraph (B), accompanying the individual with a disability provided that space for these additional individuals is available on the paratransit vehicle carrying the individual with a disability and that the transportation of such additional individuals will not result in a denial of service to individuals with disabilities. For purposes of clauses (i) and (ii) of subparagraph (A), boarding or disembarking from a vehicle does not include travel to the boarding location or from the disembarking location.

(2) Service area.—The regulations issued under this section shall require the provision of paratransit and special transportation services required under this section in the service area of each public entity which operates a fixed route system, other than any portion of the service area in which the public entity solely provides commuter bus service.

(3) Service criteria.—Subject to paragraphs (1) and (2), the regulations issued under this section shall establish minimum service criteria for determining the level of services to be required under this section.

(4) Undue financial burden limitation.—The regulations issued under this section shall provide that, if the public entity is able to demonstrate to the satisfaction of the Secretary that the provision of paratransit and other special transportation services otherwise required under this section would impose an undue financial burden on the public entity, the public entity, notwithstanding any other provision of this section (other than paragraph (5), shall only be required to provide such services to the extent that providing such services would not impose such a burden.

(5) Additional services.—The regulations issued under this section shall establish circumstances under which the Secretary may require a public entity to provide, notwithstanding paragraph (4), paratransit and other special transportation services under this section beyond the level of paratransit and other special transportation services which would otherwise be required under paragraph (4).

(6) Public participation.—The regulations issued under this section shall require that each public entity which operates a fixed route system hold a public hearing, provide an opportunity for public comment, and consult with individuals with disabilities in preparing its plan under paragraph (7).

(7) Plans.—The regulations issued under this section shall require that each public entity which operates a fixed route system—

(A) within 18 months after the effective date of this subsection, submit to the Secretary, and commence implementation of, a plan for providing paratransit and other special transportation services which meets the requirements of this section; and

(B) on an annual basis thereafter, submit to the Secretary, and commence implementation of, a plan for providing such services.

(8) Provision of services by others.—The regulations issued under this section shall—

(A) require that a public entity submitting a plan to the Secretary under this section identify in the plan any person or other public entity which is providing a paratransit or other special transportation service for individuals with disabilities in the service area to which the plan applies; and

      (B) provide that the public entity submitting the plan does not have to provide under the plan such service for individuals with disabilities.

    (9) Other provisions.—The regulations issued under this section shall include such other provisions and requirements as the Secretary determines are necessary to carry out the objectives of this section.

    (d) Review of Plan.—

    (1) General rule.—The Secretary shall review a plan submitted under this section for the purpose of determining whether or not such plan meets the requirements of this section, including the regulations issued under this section.

    (2) Disapproval.—If the Secretary determines that a plan reviewed under this subsection fails to meet the requirements of this section, the Secretary shall disapprove the plan and notify the public entity which submitted the plan of such disapproval and the reasons therefor.

    (3) Modification of disapproved plan.—Not later than 90 days after the date of disapproval of a plan under this subsection, the public entity which submitted the plan shall modify the plan to meet the requirements of this section and shall submit to the Secretary, and commence implementation of, such modified plan.

    (e) Discrimination Defined.—As used in subsection (a), the term "discrimination" includes—

    (1) a failure of a public entity to which the regulations issued under this section apply to submit, or commence implementation of, a plan in accordance with subsections (c)(6) and (c)(7);

    (2) a failure of such entity to submit, or commence implementation of, a modified plan in accordance with subsection (d)(3);

    (3) submission to the Secretary of a modified plan under subsection (d)(3) which does not meet the requirements of this section; or

    (4) a failure of such entity to provide paratransit or other special transportation services in accordance with the plan or modified plan the public entity submitted to the Secretary under this section.

    (f) Statutory Construction.—Nothing in this section shall be construed as preventing a public entity—

    (1) from providing paratransit or other special transportation services at a level which is greater than the level of such services which are required by this section,

    (2) from providing paratransit or other special transportation services in addition to those paratransit and special transportation services required by this section, or

    (3) from providing such services to individuals in addition to those individuals to whom such services are required to be provided by this section.

Sec. 224. Public Entity Operating a Demand Responsive System

If a public entity operates a demand responsive system, it shall be considered discrimination, for purposes of section 202 of this Act and section 504 of the Rehabilitation Act of 1973 (29 U.S.C. 794), for such entity to purchase or lease a new vehicle for use on such system, for which a solicitation is made after the 30th day following the effective date of this section, that is not readily accessible to and usable by individuals with disabilities, including individuals who use wheelchairs, unless such system, when viewed in its entirety, provides a level of service to such individuals equivalent to the level of service such system provides to individuals without disabilities.

Sec. 225. Temporary Relief Where Lifts Are Unavailable

(a) Granting.—With respect to the purchase of new buses, a public entity may apply for, and the Secretary may temporarily relieve such public entity from the obligation under section 222(a) or 224 to purchase new buses that are readily accessible to and usable by individuals with disabilities if such public entity demonstrates to the satisfaction of the Secretary—

(1) that the initial solicitation for new buses made by the public entity specified that all new buses were to be lift-equipped and were to be otherwise accessible to and usable by individuals with disabilities;

(2) the unavailability from any qualified manufacturer of hydraulic, electromechanical, or other lifts for such new buses;

(3) that the public entity seeking temporary relief has made good-faith efforts to locate a qualified manufacturer to supply the lifts to the manufacturer of such buses in sufficient time to comply with such solicitaion; and

(4) that any further delay in purchasing new buses necessary to obtain such lifts would significantly impair transportation services in the community served by the public entity.

(b) Duration and Notice to Congress.—Any relief granted under subsection (a) shall be limited in duration by a specified date, and the appropriate committees of Congress shall be notified of any such relief granted.

(c) Fraudulent Application.—If, at any time, the Secretary has reasonable cause to believe that any relief granted under subsection (a) was fraudulently applied for, the Secretary shall—

(1) cancel such relief if such relief is still in effect; and

(2) take such other action as the Secretary considers appropriate.

ADA Basics at a Glance

This at-a-glance checklist will help you identify existing federal rules. ADA laws will help DMCs understand the scope of work to be done and are useful for planning, budgeting, and implementation of any program. The checklist is based on Part 1192—Americans with Disabilities Act (ADA) Accessibility Guidelines for Transportation Vehicles.

Vehicle lift or *Design lift*—The design load of the lift shall be at least 600 pounds.

Platform barriers—The lift platform shall be equipped with barriers to prevent any of the wheels of a wheelchair or mobility aid from rolling off the platform during its operation.

Platform gaps—Any openings between the platform surface and the raised barriers shall not exceed 5/8 inch in width.

Boarding direction—The lift shall permit both inboard and outboard facing of wheelchair and mobility aid users.

Priority seating signs—Each vehicle shall contain sign(s) which indicate that seats in the front of the vehicle that are priority sets for persons with disabilities, and that other passengers should make such seats available to those who wish to use them.

Lighting—Any stepwell or doorway immediately adjacent to the driver shall have, when the door is open, at least 2 foot-candles of illumination measured on the step tread or lift platform.

Public information system—Vehicles in excess of 22 feet in length, used in multiple-stop, fixed-route service, shall be equipped with a public address system permitting the driver, or recorded or digitized human speech messages, to announce stops and provide other passenger information within the vehicle.

Destination and route signs—Where destination or route information is displayed on the exterior of a vehicle, each vehicle shall have illuminated signs on the front and boarding sides of the vehicle.

Restrooms—If an accessible restroom is provided, it should be designed so as to allow a person using a wheelchair or mobility aid to enter and use such restroom. The minimum clear floor area should be 35 inches (890 mm) by 60 inches (1525 mm).

Doors, Steps and Thresholds

Slip resistance—All aisles, steps, floor areas where people walk and floors in securement locations shall have slip-resistant surfaces.

All step edges shall have a band of color(s) running the full width of the step which contrasts from the step tread and riser, either dark-on-light or light-on-dark. The greatest readability is usually achieved through the use of light-colored characters or symbols on a dark background.

Doors shall have a minimum clear width when open of 30 inches (760 mm), measured from the lowest step to a height of at least 48 inches (1220 mm), from which point they may taper to a minimum width of 18 inches (457 mm). The clear width may be reduced by a maximum of 4 inches (100 mm) by protrusions of hinges or other operating mechanisms.

Planning a Pre- or Post-Convention Tour

In planning a pre- or post-convention tour, the following components must be considered:

- Hotel Selection
  - Select appropriate location.
  - Know your budget.
  - Determine whether the hotel has a commissionable rate.
  - Discover and confirm amenities.
  - Find out if continental or full breakfast is included in the room cost.
  - Determine complimentary or discounted rate for group escort.
- Meals
  - Determine which meals will be included.
  - Select off-site restaurants.
  - Arrange for choice of entrée when possible.
- Transportation
  - Determine what means of transportation will be used:
    - Motorcoach
    - Train (Request that the group be seated together.)
    - Airplane (Request that the group be seated together.)
  - Provide luggage ID tags.
  - Offer meet and greet Services if applicable.
  - Address luggage handling (including at the hotel) issues.
- Local DMC or Tour Company
  - Determine which company best suits your needs through ADME members, referrals or local convention center recommendations.
  - Tours need to be priced per person—determine minimum requirements if using contracted motorcoach services.

249

- Provide *day-to-day itinerary* with description for the promotional materials to be sent to convention attendees. Many times the client requesting the pre- or post-convention tours will include this information along with the convention information to their attendees.
- Provide an escort/guide to accompany the group.
- Costing
  - Show costing based on both double and single occupancy.
  - Include gratuity to escort, driver, and step-on guides and all applicable taxes.
  - If using over-the-road motorcoaches, cost from transportation company does not usually include the driver's lodging. This does not need to be at the same hotel, but you are responsible for securing hotel accommodations for the driver. Many restaurants will comp driver's meals and, in some cases, the escort's, if the restaurant is used for the group's function.
  - Total all costs. You will need to determine the minimum number required to guarantee the tour. This number is usually determined by the cost of a motorcoach or a minimum tour requirement. Divide the minimum number into the cost for a per-person figure.

Convention Child Care Analysis

KiddieCorp, Inc. San Diego, California
Christine Tempesta, President

KiddieCorp is the oldest national provider of convention child care. It was founded in 1986 and managed its first program in San Diego when, out of desperation, an insurance company called it to organize a children's event taking place the next evening at the San Diego Marriott & Marina. Until that time, KiddieCorp just consulted with corporations to bring childcare to its employees.

After the San Diego program, the service took off. The San Diego Convention & Visitors Bureau was very supportive and started assisting with inbound conventions. The convention groups then asked KiddieCorp to repeat its services the following year.

Until KiddieCorp came on the scene as a full-service child care provider, associations and meeting and event planners had been planning child care themselves. Chris Tempesta, president of KiddieCorp, says that their service is like any type of meeting except their attendees are children.

WHAT MADE YOU DECIDE TO FOCUS ON CHILDREN'S PROGRAMS?

KiddieCorp loved evolving into a one-of-a-kind company. They enjoyed the complete control of the policies and procedures and it was obvious that there was definitely a need for a company specializing in professional group child care. Owner/President Tempesta always adored children and had previous experience working with children. If her name were to be associated with children, it would be of the utmost importance to make sure they were safe and still having a great time. Tempesta asked her dad for advice on starting her own business. He helped her develop a service that would fulfill corporate needs while keeping families together when there was business travel. Her father passed away several years ago, and his legacy lives on at KiddieCorp.

DO YOU TRAVEL FOR PROGRAMS?

Yes, we have a team in place for all programs. Program managers have developed very successful protocol.

Clients want flexibility and reliability in our working relationship. They expect and demand good communication. It is the company's mission to make sure that every client feels that its program is first and foremost in our attention, while bending and stretching to accommodate its changing needs. In the middle of programs, managers may be asked to open early the next morning, accept 20 extra children, or add a tour on the last day of the program. As with any DMC, we need to react quickly to requests.

Our training program (called KiddieCorp U) consists of an interactive, entertaining two-hour session utilizing visual aids to stress important issues. Employees are then tested on their knowledge.

HOW IS YOUR STAFF TRAINED?

KiddieCorp trains every team member thoroughly before they begin working, and hosts a three-day workshop every year for all of their managers.

HOW DO YOU QUALIFY YOUR STAFF?

KiddieCorp maintains contacts with universities and preschools to recruit staff to work part-time with the flexibility to accommodate our unique schedule. There is a thorough application and screening procedure administered by the recruiting department.

ARE THERE ANY GOVERNMENT REGULATIONS ABOUT CHILD CARE PROGRAMS?

Usually, regulations vary state by state. Several of the KiddieCorp programs have been licensed by the particular state where the program happens. However, there are no regulations for temporary programs. Some states, like Illinois, give exemption from licensing if the company meets certain criteria. Besides the limited regulations, common sense should always prevail regarding safety and experience. For example, KiddieCorp always tries to put children on the lower or ground floor for easy evacuation.

HAVE YOU SEEN CHANGES IN CHILDREN'S PROGRAMS OVER THE YEARS?

The major change that we have seen is a wider range of ages participating. Most of our programs had previously focused on children 6 to 12 years old. Now we are doing more teen programs and infant/toddler programs. Older children are more traveled and more sophisticated, so it is important to keep up with more exciting activities that appeal to their generation. Parents seem to be more focused on where their children are and exactly what they are doing.

WHAT ARE POPULAR CHILDREN'S ACTIVITIES?

Themed activities like "Camp Out with KiddieCorp" are very popular. Children get a backpack with binoculars and a water bottle, play in a tent, and take adventure walks while pretending to see rare creatures like snipes. Anything at the beach is popular, such as lei making or group games like musical beach towels.

HOW DO YOU DEAL WITH RISK MANAGEMENT AND SECURITY?

Would I, without hesitation, put my two boys, two and four years old, in our program? Absolutely. Qualified staff, real training programs, proper supply selection, a safe room set-up, program control, and having good check-in/check-out procedures all contribute to a safe program.

We always have the same managers watching the hallway leading to the program. We even position our desks outside of the playrooms so that we can see everyone coming and going. We get all authorizations in writing and ask for identification. We record the time children are picked up and compare signatures. Family photos are taken and the photos are checked before releasing any child. Managers constantly supervise and monitor rooms and maintain security.

We maintain $5 million liability insurance, and we are happy to add clients, other DMCs, hotels, and so on, to our policy.

Meeting Contract Process Outline

Speaker
Barbara Dunn, Esq., Howe and Hutton, Ltd.

Part 1: How Do We Start? Beginning the Contract and Meeting Process

Overview—how to organize, attack, consider, and negotiate the best deal for your organization—a systematic approach to meeting contract management

- Vocabulary, terms, clauses, & conditions: understanding the framework of a contract
- Contracts versus agreements versus proposals: what's the difference?
- Understand legalities and liabilities: Good Faith/Samaritan law, the difference between negligence and gross negligence, ADA, civil rights, and consumption
- Red flags: contract caveats
- Develop your meeting contract timeline: what needs to be signed by whom by when and in what order

Part 2: Where Will We Go? Stage I in the Evolution of Meeting Contracts (4+ years out from meeting)

- Retainer: Select your legal team early
- Convention & visitors bureau contracts
- Convention center contracts
- Leases versus licenses
- Space considerations
- Indemnification
- Rights of cancellation
- Right of entry and ejection
- Quiet enjoyment
- Hotel contracts
- Cancellation
- Attrition
- Commissionable rates and rebates
- Ownership and management
- Construction
- Strikes
- Deterioration
- Financial difficulties
- Force majeure
- Risk Management and insurance policies
- Cancellation insurance: how it can save you from a financial disaster

Part 3: What Do We Need? Stage II & Stage III—Selecting Services (16–6 months out from meeting)

- Determine your need: What types of services will enhance your meeting?
- Types of services (and contracts): Each require specific contract clauses and should be signed by a certain date—can you determine what they are and when that is?
- Advertising/marketing
- Audiovisual

- Destination management companies
- Entertainment
- Exhibitors
- Housing management
- Interpretation
- Outside venues
- Speakers and speakers bureaus
- Temporary employment
- Tradeshow
- Transportation
- Negotiate what you need and what you want
- Know what you have to provide and when you could be breaking the law

Part 4: What Are We Going to Do Now? Stage IV—Party's Over and Reality Sets In

- Music licensing
- Things didn't go as planned: what happens now?
- Sifting through the paperwork: what you need to keep "just in case"
- Mediations and litigation: what happens in a mediation and what to expect
- The convention center's ceiling caved in—and there's nothing in the contract! What happens now?
- The difference between contracts and facility policy
- Looking to next year: reevaluating your meeting contract process and starting it all over again

APPENDIX 11

Ethics Quiz

The following questionnaire will ask you several questions about your behavior. The second part addresses this issue: Even if you chose to violate some of these values or rules, do you believe in the rules?

		Is not violating this value important to you?

Would you ever......

Lie to a client in order to avoid the person?
- ○ Yes
- ○ No

- ○ Yes
- ○ A little
- ○ No

Not return money from a client that gave you more than you were due?
- ○ Yes
- ○ No

- ○ Yes
- ○ A little
- ○ No

Pretend to be sick at work when you were not?
- ○ Yes
- ○ No

- ○ Yes
- ○ A little
- ○ No

Copy and use software on your computer that you did not purchase?
- ○ Yes
- ○ No

- ○ Yes
- ○ A little
- ○ No

Purchase a product or service from a discounter vendor after receiving extensive help from another vendor?
- ○ Yes
- ○ No

- ○ Yes
- ○ A little
- ○ No

Accept cash from a hotel to recommend and sell their property to a client?
- ○ Yes
- ○ No

- ○ Yes
- ○ A little
- ○ No

Knowingly accept a proposal that was written by another company and charge your client less for the same thing?
- ○ Yes
- ○ No

- ○ Yes
- ○ A little
- ○ No

Accept a supplier's gift in exchange for business not in the best interest of the client?
- ○ Yes
- ○ No

- ○ Yes
- ○ A little
- ○ No

Knowingly interfere with legal and contractual rights of others?
- ○ Yes
- ○ No

- ○ Yes
- ○ A little
- ○ No

Not report an office theft by another employee?
- ○ Yes
- ○ No

- ○ Yes
- ○ A little
- ○ No

Put a false statement in your resume to get the job?
- ○ Yes
- ○ No

- ○ Yes
- ○ A little
- ○ No

Take a complimentary familiarization trip to an area that you had no intention of using?
- ○ Yes
- ○ No

- ○ Yes
- ○ A little
- ○ No

Index

special services *(continued)*
 staffing, 151–154
 technology support, 156
specified public transportation, defined, 45
spreadsheets, software programs, 180, 182
staffing, special services, 151–154
staff-to-child ratios, child care programs, 70–72
staging, motorcoach shuttle system, 39
stanchions, motorcoach shuttle system, 40
standby vehicles, VIP transportation services, 34
station service style, food and beverage, 121
step-on guide service, tour support staff, 56
strike requirements, on-site venues, special events, 101
support staff, tours, 56
systems software, 180. *See also* software programs

technical tours, described, 52–53
technology, 175–190. *See also* electronic business; electronic
 registration
 ethics and, 208–210
 hardware, 184–186
 Internet, 186–187
 networking, 186
 pricing strategies, 161
 security and safety, 188–189
 software programs, 179–183
 special services, 156
 Technology Revolution, 176–179
 telecommunications, 187–188
 Web sites, 187
teen hospitality suites, child care programs, 65
telecommunications, technology, 187–188
Tempesta, Christine, 251–254
tentative holds, tours, 57
Tetschner, Stacy, 67
themed refreshment breaks, food and beverage, 118
Thompson, Gordon, 137
Thompson, Sam, 139
tour operators, described, 54–55
tours, 49–61
 costs of, 51, 57, 58
 creation of, 56–58
 electronic registration, 58–59, 85–88
 marketing and branding of, 51–52
 planning of, checklist for, 249–250
 professional support staff, 56
 purpose of, 50–51
 registration, 58–60

selection of, 51
types of, 52–56
traffic authorities, motorcoach shuttle system, 40
tram, defined, 45–46
transportation services, 31–48
 airport transfer, 34–37
 airport transportation proposal, 40–41
 American with Disabilities Act (ADA) of 1990, 46,
  237–245
 arrival day operations, 43–44
 bus chartering, checklist for, 227–229
 bus safety, resources for, 231–236a
 contracts, 41–42
 importance of, 32–33
 inbound transfer, 42–43
 motorcoach shuttle system, 37–40
 vehicles, 44–46
 VIP services, 33–34
Travel Industry Association of America (TIAA), 66
travel insurance programs, described, 55
travel-related tours, described, 54–55
turn-down service, gifts and amenities, 151
turn time, transportation services, 42

U.S. driver qualifications, 234–235
U.S. Motor Carrier regulations, 233–234
unlicensed sales, liquor law, 133

values, ethics, 206
vans, airport transfer services, 36
vegans, menu planning, 116
vegetarians, menu planning, 116
vehicles, transportation services, 44–46
venue manager, motorcoach shuttle system, 39
VIP services
 additional services, 146–148
 transportation, 33–34

Wagner, Elaine, 181
walking tours, described, 52
weather back-up plans, off-site venues, special events, 101
Web sites, technology, 187. *See also* electronic business;
 electronic registration; technology
wine service, 129–130
wire transfers, tours registration, 86–87
word processing, software programs, 180

Zipf, Kate, 144.